Blaby The

CW01501722

Life and times
lad in the 1950's - 1960's
J S Morey

First published in Great Britain 2018 in READ MY SHORTS; Revised 2020 and 2024 Copyright © 2024 by John Morey; All rights reserved. ISBN: 9798863088488
The moral right of the author has been asserted.

Further reading:
The series 'Love should never be this hard':
Book 1: The Sign of the Rose
Book 2: The Black Rose of Blaby
Book 3: Rose: The Missing Years
Book 4: Finding Rose
Wild Hearts Roam Free: modern western set in Wyoming
Wild Hearts Come Home: Bk 2 in the WILD HEARTS series
Unresolved? - short story linked to 'Wild Hearts Roam Free'

Those Italian Girls – set in the hills of Tuscany
Read My Shorts – short stories and poems with a message
Three Easy Pieces - Easy to read short stories

Wood-Spirit - an anthology of poems about trees
visit www.newnovel.co.uk

When I'm gone, you'll always find me in my words.

Meanwhile...

if my eyes could speak, this is what they would say.

CONTENTS

FOREWORD

To put the record straight, by referring to Blaby as 'the lost village' the author is, of course, drawing the reader's attention to *the parts* of Blaby that have been *eroded* over the years.

As far as memory allows, this is offered as a true account of a range of features, factors and events related to village life of that time.

These include over-arching social conditions, community characteristics, conventions, the economy, trade and transport, as well as some unique elements and events that made Blaby what it was - all blended to provide insight into *what it was like to live* during the first twenty five years after WW2.

Above all it is a *very personal reflection* on how the above qualities and values affected one person - the author - *at the time*. In some cases, much longer.

All parts and people mentioned are recalled with a great deal of *fondness* - not merely sentimental nostalgia. As an era, it encapsulated great times - for Britain as a nation and for British people rebuilding its infrastructure after the war.

All those specifically mentioned were good people, creating a village environment in which *it was a good place to live*.

Call this book a celebration if you will.

Looking back, there was a lot to celebrate and, wherever you looked, things were getting better.

Hopefully a lot of what came out of those times

survives today but, if you grew up during the years covered in this account you would certainly consider living *then* - and living in Blaby - a privilege.

They were unique.

Finally, the style in which this is written and presented. Apologies if it comes across as too personal and therefore self-indulgent. But, in its defence, it is hoped that something of the *flavour* of those times will filter through, as should happen with all personal memoirs.

If any of this flavour and context fails to make it through then it may be because the bridge between then and now - a span of some seventy odd years - is just too wide.

For instance, if they come over as being gentler times then perhaps they were. But we must exclude WW2 in that reference because that event was, as are all wars, savage and anything but 'gentle'. There was also a degree of censorship across the media, blocking out graphic violence and references to it - unlike the present day, of course, with such restrictions lifted.

Should such realism be allowed through? That must be a debate for another time. The account that follows in unashamedly a feel-good read.

Feel free to enjoy it as such.

Prologue - THE CHANGING YEARS

There's nothing new in saying we are a product of our environment; *the child being the father of the man* and all that. Being born soon after WW2 may not have seemed like a privilege at the time – on the surface it was a time of austerity, doing without or "making do".

For me, looking back at such rich memories, it was a pure delight. Granted, there was always the 'living in fear' bit, fear that the terrors of war could easily return. Stories of true horror were still fresh in the memory of our elders and betters (betters? - now there's a term you never hear nowadays) - remaining part of daily conversation for our parents and older siblings.

In reality, only adults *actually experienced* and had the authority to share these accounts in any detail. Nevertheless, they still to permeated down to create a general mood affecting all ages, and influencing lives across all generations.

Including my own.

Such was the background to my early years and those of my family. It shaped our attitudes and values.

It was also a time of change.

These changes were both material and the spiritual, negative as well as positive affecting our daily lives. They shaped our views on class, religion, patriotism, career aspirations, the place of women in society, our status in society and in the wider world.

It included our relationships with our neighbours

and our bosses - within our community as well as within our own family.

The one thing it didn't change was the ability and willingness of countries - still - to go to war.

Even as I speak.

Later documentaries also depict a time when everyone pulled together during, as well as after, the war. As youngster, we weren't involved in that part. But nevertheless we experienced the effect of that natural instinct. It surfaced as a feel-good, warm feeling that cloaked all that was going on at the time, as long as you had a roof over your head and food on the table.

Not everyone enjoyed even those privileges however, nor the one most important feature that rose above all else in terms of ensuring we grew up safe and well. That was family.

I was lucky enough to enjoy that in abundance.

Chapter One - MY OWN FAMILY

I loved my parents so much, even in my early 20's I couldn't imagine life without them.

They had me late in their lives. In their forties. I like to think I was a tangible celebration once the miseries off WW2 were over. Mortality was closer for them than it was for the parents of other children I knew. But they were still the foundation for the love and caring within the family that infused the values of my brother and sisters. I would like to think that some of it rubbed off on me too for later life. It wasn't over-sentimentality.

There was an honesty about it.

Both my parents worked hard. Dad was skilled and educated; Mam was semi-skilled as a factory machinist in the shoe trade. My earliest recollections of her are as a home-worker - until I was able to start school, at which point she was released to go to work in a factory. But working at home was a popular option after the war for those with pre-school children. She was not the sort to sit down idly and read a book. Nor was there was TV at that time unless you were part of the super-rich, so watching a celebrity chef programme - Fanny Cradock or Philip Harben - was a non-starter.

Or unless you lived in America.

Nor did she bother with women's social groups like the WI. Instead, when she was not *earning* a living, she would be *saving* money: darning our socks instead of buying new ones (like today), knitting clothes - or altering my older brother's clothes *to fit me.*

She even bought wool in the cheapest way possible, in a skein and not already in a convenient ball. I remember complaining when she asked me to hold my 6-year-old arms out to hold a skein of wool, so that she could wind it into a ball, ready to knit.

It would be a familiar scene at at the time, leading to a very strong dependence I formed with my mother. Because mam was at home and both Brian and Betty would be at school most of the time, I had her all to myself. This made me somewhat possessive (which I talk about a little later on). On the plus side, it left me with an impression that everything around me was warm and safe both emotionally and physically.

Which it was. Sort of.

Not only that, although untrue from meteorological perspectives, every *day* seemed to be warm and sunny. The house was always warm thanks to a roaring open coal fire. This doubled as a means to dry clothes in the winter, or to make toast - holding a slice of bread in front of flames using a brass toasting fork.

A thick hand-cut slice; and white bread.

Dad must have provided for us all very well, but this wasn't always the case for lots of post-war families. Only until well after such times did it become evident that there were communities living in real poverty, with a daily battle against cold, damp housing, meagre diet, insecure job prospects, and ill health.

This was especially true of inner cities, not just

London, Manchester and Birmingham, but also places like Nottingham, a mere thirty miles away.

Leicester seems to have always been immune from such extremes to a degree, being at the hub of major transport links, leaders in small industry (e.g. Corah's being the largest clothing manufacturer in Europe going back decades), and not over-dependant on single large industries, with their attendant economic vulnerabilities, such as the coal and steel communities.

That was the over-arching economic context of the day, but let's return to how it affected us as a more human left.

Dad must have worked hard and, possible long hours. That may be why I don't recall much about dad at that time, apart from the feeling that he was always cross with me when he *was* around. Or maybe I was too close to make, which made me too soft. He would shout at me and, when a little older, give me a clout - which he called 'boxing my ears' - if I deserved it. He would later say that "I was a mistake" and that he would "put me in a home" if I misbehaved.

But he didn't actually mean it.

Did he...?

Times were hard for the head of the family as far as feeding four hungry mouths - six with mam and dad. So no; I prefer to think he never meant it. I was a safety valve. And, just to be clear, it was a slap - *definitely no punching or bruising* - and certainly not abuse.

Just discipline.

And he never touched the girls or my mam.

Apparently he was a travelling representative - a commercial traveller, as they were called - for Singer sewing machines. That's why he never seemed to be around except at weekends, often coming home after I had gone to bed. It also explains how we came to have a Singer sewing machine in the house, enabling mam to earn valuable housekeeping *at home* to help support four children.

My brother Brian was seven years older than me and I have no recollection of him, or had no real connection with him - *in those early years.* We didn't seem to connect in any way but we must have shared a bedroom. I have this vague recollection of a striped mattress filled with horse hair, that mam had to redistribute equally within the mattress, every week or so, to prevent it being lumpy. It sat on a base with iron springs. My sisters Joan and Betty also shared a room. As hinted at earlier, I must also have shared his clothes when he outgrew them – a common feature of family life in those days.

"Hand-me-downs".

Betty was five years older than Brian and bright. She won a scholarship to Lutterworth Grammar School unlike her older sister Joan - older by another five years - who went to the secondary modern school in south Wigston. It meant a long school day for Betty. Lutterworth was eight miles away, to which she probably travelled on a school bus unless dad was able to take her in his Singer car.

(Provided *by* Singer, but it may also have *been* a Singer car - a leading British brand of the day.)

Needless to say, I recall nothing of Betty at a personal level from early years pre-school and later – at least not until I was at secondary school age.

Except for one vague memory.

It must have been in her summer end of term when the school had an open day, or a sports day. Apart from Joan, who had started work by then, the whole family arrived at a field on a lovely summer's day, a field bedecked with white marquees, tents, bunting and flags. There may also have been horses and a gymkhana, given that some of the other girls may have been rich, with parents who could afford *to pay* for their daughter to go to grammar school. Most of all, again that 'warmth' has filtered down over the years whenever I recall that day - that solitary one day - that has stayed with me.

It was also typical of how grammar school shaped Betty's life in a good way inasmuch as she became different from us - better mannered and better spoken.

She would grow up to be 'posh'.

Joan was five years older than Betty, and worked at Griffin & Gamble in their factory, I believe as a machinist. My impression was that she worked hard, was fast and earned quite good money. I noticed this about her more, later on in life, in that she was always a busy person, doing or making something, and always at a pace, never languid and slow.

She was driven then, and throughout her whole life.

Looking back, and in the context of the day, that made sense. Women had been liberated by the war when they had to step into men's shoes and do men's jobs. (e.g. my aunt Rowena even drove bread van in the war). Those years of austerity left people like my sister with an urgency to make hay while the sun shone, to appreciate employment opportunities, and to earn the money if it was there to be earned.

The war had left the country with a massive debt to America, and a massive rebuilding programme was underway, not just to replace the bombed communities and factories, but to introduce a social framework and game-changing services like the NHS - free at the point of access, but paid for by national insurance. The latter was only possible if the population was in full employment, hence a period of real growth.

I didn't appreciate it then, but over time I became increasingly proud of Joan in so many ways - her will to 'get on in life', her honesty and respect for every one, but she also had a great sense of fun. The country needed people like Joan; with her attitude.

'A proper working class Gel!' Gold dust!

But why not? All that must have come through from mam and dad. We were fortunate to live in a household of over-whelming love for each other. Ironically we never said out loud that we loved each other, and never kissed each other hello or goodbye.

That was for softies - or for posh people.

The exception was mam and dad, who would exchange kisses when dad went off to work. Otherwise neither ever told any of us that they loved us, nor did any of us tell each other we loved each other. We didn't need to.

We just knew.

For us, love manifested itself when it was required, when the occasion presented itself. As a small boy, sister Betty would comfort me if she felt that dad had shouted at me unfairly; on another front, even much later as a teenager I would get the occasional pomegranate (yes!) from Joan on a Saturday.

I loved her for that. No big deal, you may say, but those small kindnesses spoke volumes then, as they do now. Some things you never forget.

Although Dad was strict when it came to respect, manners, and general behaviour, he was supportive. I appreciated his encouragement if I did well at school; mam was always kind. This next instance was typical of the sacrifices she made for me out of love.

It happened like this.

It was just before the new school term. High school. I must have been about 13 years old – the age when you become self-conscious about your appearance. Peer pressure. Fitting in with the rest.

And the subject in question now?

I needed a new top coat for the winter.

The norm was a navy blue regulation gabardine raincoat and, if it was cold, you just put on an extra layer. A jumper or a vest. Simple! But I had spotted this raglan-sleeved light brown overcoat when we were in Leicester, mam and I, shopping. It was perfect. The problem was it was half as expensive again as the raincoat.

So what? I wanted it.

Mam explained all this to me outside the shop where I'd seen it in the window as we passed by. It wasn't her normal shop, or Lamberts Wholesalers She explained that she'd budgeted for the normal raincoat whereas the one I wanted was well above the price range. But I, selfishly, was insistent. I wanted *that* coat in the window. It was late Saturday afternoon, in Leicester, in winter, and getting dark.

I can see it all now.

I was told to stay outside while mam went in to explain things to the male shop assistant. I've no idea what was said but, whatever it was, it worked. He was nodding. I was so thrilled when he took it out of the window, not knowing - nor really caring at the time - what mam had to sacrifice to afford it. I found out later they'd worked out a price that was below the ticket price, which was more than she strictly "could afford", but whatever she ended up paying left her with enough – just enough – for the bus fare home.

At the time I was delighted.

However, years later - and even now - I fill up with love for my mam for the way she placed my needs, *my selfish needs*, above all else, and I realise the sacrifices she must have had to make. How many other instances of sacrifice and unselfishness on the part of my parents were there that I never even knew about?

It's too late to thank them now.

Perhaps this will serve as my apology.

Looking back, though, that attitude's the norm today. We must have it now. No bother to save. A thing called Hire Purchase was just coming in - the 'never-never' - the suggestion that you never paid of the debt. This wasn't strictly true, but it was a problem for some who might saddle themselves with too many monthly repayments, then lose their jobs.

Thank to Hire Purchase, it was so easy for the banks to introduce credit cards - a sort of 'flexible' Hire Purchase in some ways.

And now, in 2023, they want to phase out cash!

Chapter Two - LIVING IN THE AVENUE

Playing in the gutter was not as bad as it sounds.

In those days – we have to wind the clock back from the time of the story I've just told you - I guess I am talking about 1949. Village streets were pretty much devoid of cars. They were safe and clean, if you ignore the odd dollop of horse manure. 'Clean' muck.

So, too, were the gutters. Clean. People kept them that way and, by "people", I meant those who lived in our street – as well as the regular road sweeper. He was a man, not a vehicle. Not that I always welcomed the road-sweeper. He took away the "sand" in the gutter that I used to create a dam whenever the stream of rainwater cascaded down after a sudden shower.

The street, as I call it, was in fact "The Avenue". Literally. Number 5, The Avenue, Blaby. We lived in a small bungalow half way up the street (or half way down, if you were going from Enderby Road to Park Road.). It really *was* an avenue, lined with trees. I'm not sure what sort. All I do remember is that they were not ones you could climb. Their branches started way up the main trunk, and certainly out of reach for a four year old. But always, always, there were pigeons cooing within the higher branches on a warm summer's afternoon.

Here we go again. Warm feeling coating my memories.

So, you may ask, how come this small child was playing in the gutter, *on his own*, unsupervised in a mostly empty street? What dangers lurked? The reality was, and the reason I was on my own at that age – pre-school – was that as a rule you weren't into the "making friends" bit. Except for one boy - Dave Freeman. He live in one of the big houses opposite.

The other reason I was a solitary figure was because my brother was seven years older and therefore too old to be playing with little kids like me. Brian was either *at school* during the day or, at weekends, playing with *his* friends.

Usually Sammy Wale or Colin Swanwick.

My two sisters were even older, old enough to go to work. So they weren't around. Dad worked too, of course. I hardly saw him. And mam was a "home-worker" (as I mentioned earlier). That meant that she used the Singer sewing machine in the kitchen and made things – at home.

But she couldn't always be looking over me. So...

That's how I came to be playing out in the street, *on my own*, building dams for the stream of water in the gutter after a sudden shower.

I had boats, too. OK, let's call them sticks and, before you ask, "Why didn't you have real toy boats?", as I just explained, this was 1949, after the war. *The austere years*. Nothing like the so-called, relatively fake, ten years austerity the Labour Party blame the Conservatives for in 2010 onwards. There was no money for children's treats like toys unless it was

Christmas. Neither was there much money for clothes, apart from essentials, which is why I was wearing the shirt and trousers Brian had out-grown, handed down before they were worn through.

And one other thing about toys. Toy *battleships* – the kind you might think to play with in the bath as a small boy?

Forget it.

They were made of lead!

Yes. They sank! (I never did get that bit.)

Now, in the 21st Century, for many reasons, children my age wouldn't be playing in the street on their own. For one thing it wouldn't be safe. In 1949 it was. Safe from traffic, safe from some kids wanting to do you damage, safe from some adults wanting to do much worse. Not that I was neglected and on my own for hours on end. I'm sure mam was either in the front garden, or looking out the window now and again as she darned our socks.

(Don't know what 'darning' means? Google it!)

And yes, we had a front garden – as well as a back garden with fruit trees, a shed, a lawn behind which were allotments for growing fruit and vegetables - a discipline brought in after the war when food was scarce. The *front* garden was just a few feet of lawn, bordered by a privet hedge (under which I once found a dad cat), and a gate opening onto the pavement.

Next door lived Mr and Mrs Meyer. I guess they were German Jews. Refugees from the war? They had more money than we did because Mr Meyer was an optician. Please don't ask me how I worked that out at 3-4 years old. The main point about mentioning the Meyers was that Mrs Meyer used to give me sweets using their ration book. They had no children.

Ration books? Again, Google that if you're unsure. I just remember my mam thanking her for her kindness. (Though I wasn't allowed to take sweets *direct* from Mrs Meyer.)

So what other memories does a four year old store away?

As I alluded to earlier, I remember being afraid of my dad. *Why did I annoy him so much? Why did he always have to shout at me? I guess I misbehaved – but how? And why almost all of the time?*

He took that answer to his grave.

I never asked, not even in later life. Funny thing is, I was hardly aware of Brian, or sisters Betty and Joan who'd probably just discovered boys, so that could have caused a bit of friction. But Brian? I never saw him clouted. He was perfect.

He never did anything wrong.

I didn't start school until I was five. I suppose that's when I made my first real friend – Melv, although for a time there was Dave Freeman from across the street.

Dave had two elder brothers and a sister. That bit I *do* remember. But he didn't have a dad – either that or he was away a lot. Their house was bigger than ours and I recall Mrs Freeman being a bit posh.

It was in the way she spoke and dressed.

Sometimes I would go over there to play - which I

loved. I had two big reasons for going over. One, he had a rocking horse; two, a TV. They must have been *seriously loaded*. After school we'd watch Bill & Ben, Children of The New Forest, and I suppose The Cisco Kid and Andy Pandy!

Dave and I remained friends until he won a secondary school scholarship for Loughborough Art College as a boarder. Later, the family emigrated to Canada. I would love to connect with Dave one final time, but that's never going to happen.

OK, to continue. So now I must be five years old. What more memories do I have to share?

Here goes:

We skip to the time when my eldest sister, Joan, was "courting" her future husband, Derek. He came from a council house family and was an absolute diamond in every way. Initially, my dad didn't approve of this beau from 'the wrong side of the tracks' but later in life they became almost brothers. Derek was like a second dad to me by the time I got into my teens, even though initially, at five years old, I seemed always to annoy him as much as I did my real dad!

Did I have a knack for annoying people then?

(*What about now*? I hear you ask.)

My earliest recollection was to hear the 'pop-pop-pop' of his motorbike at least a mile or so down the road, as he came to pick up Joan to go on a date. I can see Joan even now, in front of the mirror in mam and dad's bedroom, getting ready to go out – hurrying as she heard the familiar sound of Derek's bike.

As I said, Betty was five years younger than Joan and went to Grammar School in Lutterworth on a scholarship. Later she was also a Sunday School teacher at Blaby Church of England church. She was a gentler spirit and her superior education had made her posh. You could tell by the way she talked - a sharp contrast to her older sister, Joan, on the other hand, who worked at Griffin and Gamble. That was the factory round the corner from where we lived – in Park Road - a walk of a hundred yards or so. (In those days they sounded a siren when it was time to clock in, and out, of the factory - a hang-over from the last war.)

As for Betty, I can see *her* now, having been walked home from Sunday School by a chap called Derek(?) Smith. She was standing on one side of the gate, with him on the other. Betty was always telling me to go away.

But why?

Then I guess he stopped calling and I found out later – when I could understand what it meant – he went to The Congo as a missionary. This was at the time the Mau Mau were killing people out in Kenya. Betty was asked to go with him but refused. Ironically, years later when Betty was in her thirties, she met a second generation white South African and eventually married him and settled over there.

She died of kidney cancer still in her early fifties.

I still miss her.

Chapter Three - I START SCHOOL

I know I've jumped around a bit but things are roughly in the order they happened.

First, Infants School.

Miss Shields was my first school teacher and was gorgeous. I was unaware who the film actress Rhonda Fleming was at this point; if I had been then there would be no doubt who Miss Shields resembled. Slim, blonde – and posh (and rich) enough to own an open-top sports car. In red. An MGA? 'Healey'? Triumph?

Possibly a Morgan.

One thing I do recall that's stayed with me. She picked up my mam from our house one day *in her sports car* to take her to vote in the national election.

To vote Tory?

(I think mam and dad were Labour; they never said.)

The voting station was in the centre of the village and we lived on the edge. Yes, the sports car *was* red. Yes, they did drive off with the hood down. And yes, my mam *did* wear a head-scarf.

Probably with a floral pattern.

As ever, for special occasions mam wore her best top coat (even though it was perhaps May) – and carried a handbag. Like the Queen. One thing about handbags in those days, they had a centre clasp – on the top, not the side - and it "snapped" as you closed it. I loved to open and close it. For long periods of time.

That may explain why I could be so annoying.

As you can imagine after so may years the events, but more especially the order they came in, tend to blur, so I will continue in an "in no particular order".

Miss Shields was a lovely person – perfect for her vocation and seeming more like another big sister, even though I bet she was barely twenty years old. Soon after I started primary school we had a new Head Teacher, Mr. Dixon. Something happened that made her almost qualify for that big sister role.

Here goes.

First, if you are still alive, Mr. Dixon, I don't actually *blame you* for what I am about to describe, even though it - and you - did have an early, negative, affect on my confidence level that stayed with me and re-emerges on occasion, even to this day.

It all started with Dr. Barnardo's and their collection for the charity supporting disadvantaged children. One day, everyone in the school was given an envelope to take home and collect whatever their parents could afford to donate. And bring it back. Sealed. The next day I gave in my envelope. It was anonymous. A day or two *later* Mr. Dixon entered the classroom.

For whatever reason we were all sat on the floor.

Taking over from Miss Shields, he went on to explain how it had come to his attention that some children had spent their donation on sweets. He then invited anyone guilty of this to raise their hand and confess. As I said, we were sat on the floor. However, I *did* have my arm resting on the desk *above me*.

Guess what?

It looked to him as if I had my hand raised.

Mr. Dixon picked me out, made me stand up and face the class, proceeding to ask me why I'd committed this heinous crime. I hadn't done anything wrong but, somehow, I was *so* intimidated that I was unable to deny it or even utter one word in my defence. Named and shamed I was told to sit down again. No action was taken against me, but the damage was done.

I stood guilty in front of the whole school.

A little later, and after Mr. Dixon had left the room, Miss Shields knelt next to me as I sat quietly, still in shock at my tiny desk. She asked me why I'd done it. Only then was I able to speak. I explained that I *hadn't* taken the money, even though I was too frightened to say so at the time. (Yes, in those days you respected your teachers without question.)

Miss Shields immediately cleared my name with the Headmaster but the experience left me scarred to this day. Over the years I've often, quite wrongly, assumed that I'm being accused when I'm not.

It's a hang-up I've had to live with.

I went to the village school, Blaby C. of E, from 1951 to 1957. So had both my sisters but much earlier. Mr. Backhouse was Headmaster in their day and he was still there for just one term when I started.

By that time he was ancient.

Over 20 years had passed.

But I still have his image ingrained in my

consciousness. Easily six foot in height, he was thin and angular and rode a large-framed black bicycle. As large as *that* was, he looked too big for it.

One thing that changed when he left was that they took out the open fireplace. (No. He didn't take it *with* him!) A roaring coal fire was such a lovely sight on a cold and frosty winter's day - yet another example of the warmth I felt in those days. But they replaced the open fire with a new boiler and extra radiators.

Another teacher who left soon after was a career spinster teacher, Miss Basham. Yes, she did have a deep voice and wore sensible shoes and, Yes, that was her real name! But she was very kind and, because she was a strong character, we felt safe with her leading us on our nature walks.

Unlike the rest of us, my brother Brian went to Whetstone Primary, the school in the next village. It was no further than where we lived in The Avenue but, because mam and Brian were able to walk across three farmland fields**, there was no main road to cross. So it was a lot safer. It wasn't until much later that I questioned mam as to why I didn't go to Whetstone or, more to the point, why Brian didn't go to the Blaby school, like his sisters and me.

"Well, I didn't want Brian to have to cross the busy Lutterworth Road to the Blaby school, in case he had an accident."

Her reply has always rested with me uneasily.

You can see why. "OK," I thought, "so whilst it's not OK for Brian to risk life and limb crossing the road, it's

OK for *me* to get squashed by an articulated lorry?"

Jeez. Was I assuming the victim again?

I mentioned that Brian had two particular friends: Sammy Wale and Colin Swanwick. They also lived in The Avenue. Like Betty, Brian didn't want little brother intruding on his social life, but on one occasion Brian relented. He allowed me to tag along on one of his rambles across nearby fields with his mates.

Quite unusually on this occasion there was a circus nearby and, although we didn't see 'The Big Top', we heard they had elephants. To this day – but very rarely, I admit – I dream of going on that walk and, whether or not it's true or part of the dream, on that ramble we come across elephant footprints.

Really?

Nah! It just cannot be true! Surely not!

** Much, much later, I was part of a Blaby gang of kids (aged say 10 to 15) who went to war with a group of similar tear-aways from Whetstone. The dispute was about the ownership of 'no-man's-land' - the field *sandwiched between* the one closest to Blaby (clearly ours) and the one closest to Whetstone (clearly theirs). Each village gang assembled at the gates at either end of the field in the middle – and threw bricks and stones at each other. Amazing! We could have been killed. Luckily, nobody was hurt. Nobody won, nobody lost.

How did it end?

We just got tired after a while and went home.

Two other instances that occurred, but without me knowing about until later, I still do remember. The first happened in the local sweet shop owned by Mabel Pegg on Enderby Road. (Yes, all she sold were sweets, usually taking ration book tokens to pay for them.) It involved my mam taking my sister Joan for a treat – or so it was supposed to be - but it ended in disaster.

She saw a Chinaman for the first time!

Seeing anything other than a white person may not seem unusual now, but then, it was a rarity - especially in Mabel Pegg's village sweet shop. Joan screamed the place down. Of course it can be an everyday event now as people from China are now fully integrated into our society. So it's not remarkable in itself, out of context, apart from highlighting the fact that then – in the 1940's and '50's – the normal village resident was so insular, so ignorant I guess you could say, and rarely exposed to any*thing* or any*one* outside of their immediate vicinity. There was radio but no TV, so other cultures rarely featured – *visually at least.*

Suffice to say it wouldn't happen now.

The second drama took place when I swallowed a sugared almond – probably bought from Mabel Pegg's – which stuck in my throat.

I stopped breathing.

I was turning blue. We were at home at the time but we had no phone. (Not everybody did, then.)

And there was no doctor nearby.

All dad could think of doing was to pick me up and run for the nearest surgery – easily a mile away. Half an hour on foot. It would have been Doctor Drury's, I guess, on the other side of the village.

He had to hurry.

Luckily he hadn't gone far before he tired – *and fell over with me in his arms*. I said 'luckily' because the *jolt* of the fall dislodged the sweet in my throat.

Dad had saved my life that day.

'We'll meet up on 'Ozzy Lane.'
'Where?'

We couldn't leave without reference to Hospital Lane.

'Ozzy Lane' led to Countesthorpe, as did Welford Road, but to the opposite end of that village. Along the former there were two highlights: The Cottage Homes and a railway line, over a bridge that is no longer there. Nor is the dip in the road. Whenever the the Soar Valley flooded, so did Hospital Lane, now and again, making it impassible.

I heard it still floods, but to a lesser extent.

For all sorts of reasons - perhaps because it was on the fringe of the village and going into the unknown - Ozzy Lane attracted us as a natural playground. But, in those days cutting across the fields to get to the spinney, unlike now, could get you into trouble with the farmer.

No idea his name; never saw him.

And if you carried on *through* the spinney you came out into the grounds of Blaby Hall with its lake, its rowing boat, and the Ice House, all of which I explored at midnight one night back in the sixties - on my way back from The Bakers Arms. I was on my own and, although it was spooky, misty, mysterious it was also fun. Spurred on by a few pints inside me I was in an adventurous mood and, even in those days, not afraid of the dark.

The setting couldn't have been more perfect. It was a crisp, moonlit night, and a veil of mist hovered a couple of feet or so above the meadow. There were cows grazing but they ignored me, so I made my way across the meadow to the lake. There was a rowing boat and, well, I'd be a fool not to. So I did. I scrambled in and pushed myself off from the bank. Grabbing both oars, within a few strokes I was in the centre of the water. That's when they must have heard me - the dogs, that is. Barking.

I saw lights go on in the big house so I made for the shore where I jumped clear and made haste for the gap in the hedge on Sycamore Street, where I'd first come in. Nobody came out, the dogs stopped barking, so I snuck out undetected. But, just as I was leaving I saw an entrance into what seemed to be a cave, an air-raid shelter kind of construction plus what might have been a gun turret. I couldn't quite make it out but it may have been the ice house.

By this time I was quite sober but, throughout, I was able to really savour the atmosphere and relish exploring the unknown. 'Behind those walls' (the high wall down Church Street and along Sycamore Road) had always been a mystery to us all as school children - a forbidden zone - so this midnight excursion was a real eye-opener. It hadn't disappointed.

Where I emerged out into Sycamore Street was just down the road from where a best friend of ours - a very clever best friend of ours - a year younger but he was so bright he skipped two years over us and was at university before we'd even taken our 'O-Level' exams. His name was Alan 'Cac-Cac' Clarke and another good friend, Richard Cobley, lived further up from him on the corner with Welford Road. That was towards Countesthorpe, just before Western Drive - a council estate at the time.

Behind Western Drive they built a housing estate on which they added another favourite pub - The Egyptian Queen. Sadly, this iconic 'theme pub', dressed in gold fixtures and fitting and depicting Cleopatra and Nefertiti, has since been pulled down. That fate was also suffered by

The Tom Thumb on the Fairway Estate (formerly Shoults' Tomato Farm) built in the '50's off Grove Road.

Thank goodness the Dog and Gun survived, but the by-pass that was threatened when we built the bungalow on Hillview Nurseries, opposite The Blaby Rose Gardens, eventually 'happened'. It ran across what was our land. The house we built was also demolished, and I can hardly bear thinking about it....

Sorry. I got a bit carried away there.

Life was sweet...Blaby's soft centre

Mrs Cherry's Sweet Shop, Sycamore Street

Mrs Cherry's sweet shop was a feature well before I went to Blaby C of E Junior School.

She enjoyed a captive clientele of young pupils with money to spend - usually a modest penny for a 'Penny Chew' or bubble gum with collectible sports cards inside!

It was a time when I recall new brands emerging. Wagon Wheels were launched, Mars Bars were popular, I became aware of Penguins for the first time, but sweets from as little as a farthing (sorry, Google that one as well) like gobstoppers, licorice and licorice root and sherbet fountains were our staple diet.

It was on the corner of Church Street, which led up to the school and the church itself, and Blaby Hall entrance.

On the other hand, Mabel Pegg's sweet shop was half a mile away. It didn't represent competition, given that most people walked. But not that far for a treat.

Mabel Pegg's Sweet Shop on Enderby Road

Mabel Pegg's was just outside the main village - a converted front room of a terraced house. It was half a mile (maybe less) into the centre of the village - the cross roads - and other shops.

She took ration vouchers for payment during and immediately after WW2. Jars of boiled sweets dominated the front window and the shelves behind the counter.

Back then there was no self-service.

Chapter Four - HILLVIEW NURSERIES

First of all, my dad - Kenneth William Sercombe Morey - founded Hillview Nurseries back in the 1950's. For the record, it was NOT started by the grandparent's of the politician, Lembick Opec, as claimed by his mother. To be fair to her, she was only about ten years old at the time when her parents bought the small market garden from my dad, back in 1954. She wouldn't be aware of such detail.

From what I can gather, the family that bought the business from us were Estonian refugees, fleeing persecution from what dad referred to as the 'Red Russians. As opposed to 'White Russians' which I think was something to do with the communist takeover and Stalin's regime of cleansing the countries under the (red) Soviet flag from dissidents.

I haven't Googled what the history books have said about all this. I'm just repeating what my dad told me. My perception was White Russians - Good; Red Russians - Bad.

Before we lived at Hillview Nurseries itself - i.e. before we built a bungalow there - I remember my mam taking me along to what we called 'the field'. We lived at the time *in* the village in The Avenue.

Situated opposite Blaby Rose Gardens, the market garden, aka nursery, aka small-holding, was about a mile outside the village along the main Lutterworth Road. That was one of the main routes from Leicester to London, as I understand, before the introduction of the M1 (and other American-style highways).

In short, quite a trek for a four year old. Me. Before we moved out there, mam and I walked all the way from the village on a hot summer's day to join dad as he toiled in the fields. This would be about mid-day; he had probably been working out there on his own - albeit accompanied by our collie-cross, Bob, all morning. We took him welcome refreshments, usually sandwiches and a bottle of tea.

Note I said *bottle* of tea.

Thermos flasks were expensive. We made do with an empty lemonade bottle to be filled with hot tea – *carefully* filled with the boiling liquid without cracking – and wrapped in a towel to keep it hot until we arrived after our half an hour walk. As I recall, the milk was already added! (How do I remember all this?)

We just had the one dog at the time, the long-haired black & white collie cross (Bob). We all loved him. *Everyone* loved Bob. He became my dog later on until he died aged 13 years. I can still recall him, a long-haired collie panting in the summer heat, following me wherever I went. That was until one day when he just took himself off to lay in the ditch opposite our house - by which time we lived back in the village - to die.

Dad found him.

He never could understand how pure instinct took him to where Bob had decided to slope off undetected to rest his weary bones for that last time. For reasons even dad couldn't explain, he decided to look under the hedgerow opposite our house, after worrying when Bob failed to come home that night from his rambles.

Anyway, back on the farm - sorry - small-holding...

Occasionally we were caught in a thunder storm right out there in the countryside. There was no shelter before we had the bungalow built, so we snuggled under the thick hawthorn hedgerow that ran between our land and Bert Attfield's. Sometimes we would misread the weather forecast and were caught out without waterproof coats.

We had to make do.

In those days, crops of cabbages, peas, Brussel sprouts and cauliflower were harvested and gathered initially into jute "sack bags". Later the contents were transferred into specially made 'bushel boxes' for transport to market.

These sack bags were also useful for many things, in our case, keeping the rain off. We made capes out of them by tucking one corner into its opposite to make a hood, which we then draped over our head.

They were *almost* waterproof!

Another use for them I found out later, came in when we had a young border collie bitch - company for Bob; Bess. She was also a Border Collie 'cross', but short-haired. As a pup she suffered from fits. Dad was unsure of the cause; he speculated it might have been the stress of being carried by my sister Joan's lap on the back of Derek's motorbike when she fetched Bess from the farm. But Dad knew the solution.

And it wasn't tablets.

When Bess would "fit", she'd run and run around the 10-acre smallholding until she simply just got tired. Then dad would be able to catch her and, with Bess still fitting but less severely now, he'd gentle her as he put her into a sack bag - where she was kept quiet.

After a while she would be fine.

Dad's natural of love and caring for animals always showed itself on occasions like that. Eventually, Bess stopped having fits altogether, living to the old age of thirteen and, on the way, giving us two litters of pups.

They were hers and Bob's.

To this day I remember her pups – first a litter of seven, then of six – running round the garden, one behind the other in a line following after me. I also recall my instructions I had to follow just before and immediately after Bess had her litter. Dad warned me not to disturb Bess when she was at the point of giving birth – which took place in a dark airing cupboard just off the kitchen near the boiler.

If threatened at birthing, she might eat them!

Once they were weaned we advertised in the Leicester Mercury and sold them; dogs were twenty one shillings (about one pound or a dollar fifty each), bitches a little less at eighteen shillings and sixpence. I was sad to see them go but we needed the money, not more dog mouths to feed.

Once the bungalow was built we moved out of the village. I suddenly realised how lonely it was - with no Dave Freeman living opposite and, because siblings were either at school all day or had started working, no sisters or brother. So Bess became my dog and my best friend until she died.

Hit by a lorry on the Lutterworth Road.

It was winter-time and therefore dark at five o'clock when we heard that fateful knock on the back door. We opened the door only to see a man holding this dark, lifeless shape cradled in his arms.

Whether he was the driver who'd knocked her over I'm not sure. He worked for the British Road Services whose depot was close to the Dog and Gun pub at Whetstone Gorse. I guess they worked on Saturdays - which was the day she was killed. If it was him then a belated 'Thank-you' for delivering our faithful Bess to us that night. It would be hard for anyone to see her dark shape and, although it wasn't illegal to let a dog wander in those days, I guess we had to accept out share of the blame.

She was thirteen; it was her time.

The bungalow and Hillview Nurseries land was where the Blaby by-pass is now. Even when dad's planning permission was granted the new road was on the planning department's forward plans, somewhere. In the end the preferred route took it across our 10-acre nursery. Just after the war and even when dad first bought the land, there was some restriction on being able to build a home on the site.

Dad fought the restriction and a compromise was reached - he eventually managed obtain consent to build a bungalow *on the far corner* of the land, furthest away from the existing main Lutterworth Road to which the by-pass would later be linked.

The earliest recollection of our new home was a realisation of how primitive, initially, our living was. When we moved in there was no gas and perhaps no electric. Luckily it was summer, I guess, because I vividly recall mam cooking on an open fire – *outdoors* - in what was to become our back garden!

We pioneered the outdoor barbecue in the UK!

It was 1950.

All four children were still living at home then, including Joan who was seventeen years older than me. She would be twenty one - old enough to get married when she wanted without needing parental consent. I don't remember her actual wedding day, but it must have been just after we moved out there. In the meantime, instead of a three-minute nip round the corner, Joan would now have to walk, I guess, the mile or so to the factory in the village where we used to live.

Joan and Derek bought a house in Shakespeare Street, Aylestone, with Joan working locally as a machinist. Derek was a window cleaner. He worked hard - as did Joan - so that by their early forties they paid off their mortgage, moving to the Isle of Wight to buy and run a guest house by the early 1970's.

Betty was also working, at just 16 years old in 1950. She'd started out as an apprentice dressmaker – I think in Leicester – but it didn't work out. To this day I remember mam and dad consoling her when she came home one day, early, apparently having been "let go" by her employers. She was so distraught. I remember dad comforting her the day it happened.

Parents' unconditional love like that stayed with me.

So that's how Betty moved on with a career change to become a shorthand-typist, then secretary at English Electric. There, quite some time after, and not until she was in her thirties, she married Denys, an engineer on secondment from South Africa.

Anyway, back to the then present; Betty thrived in the office environment. It was a larger company - English Electric - originally called Power Jets. Sir Frank Whittle developed the jet engine there in WW2 before he left for America. I mention that because we could still hear the turbines being tested when we lived at Hillview Nurseries. The testing site was only a mile and a half away, across (Farmer) Bert Attfield's land, which stretched from our place into neighbouring Whetstone. It seemed closer at the time.

Our modest three-bedroom bungalow was otherwise quiet and cosy, with Joan and Betty sharing initially but not for long, as did Brian and me. But not long after we'd moved to Hillview Nurseries, Joan left to marry Derek. As I said, I remember nothing of the wedding.

What I do recall about those times, however, was that I was a very clinging child – very attached to my mam. "Mardy" was the local dialectic term for my unreasonable behaviour. Sulky, but loud with it. I admit I was a real pain. They called me spoilt because I was the youngest. Just to give you some idea how pathetic I was, just a 10-minute walk from Hillview Nurseries was the Dog and Gun pub, next door to the British Road Services and the Anstey Nomads cricket ground.

Mam and dad liked to go to the pub occasionally, usually at the weekend. There was no TV for entertainment, merely a radio, and any village activity was always too far away after a hard days' work. The pub was a n easy option. The *only* option. That's when I always kicked off – screaming and crying and generally being a right pain for my sisters and brother the whole time, until mam and dad returned.

Only then would I stop. I really was pathetic.

I also remember I had measles soon after the move - perhaps around 1951. I'd already recovered from whooping cough, but I don't recall even having that. As for other childhood diseases, I didn't have chicken pox until my forties!

The reason I mention measles is two-fold:

One, I remember the taste of the medicine – which was not half bad taste-wise; two, Doctor Drury *made home visits* certainly unheard of nowadays.

The National Health Service was in its infancy.

But it worked!

We lasted four years at Hillview Nurseries with my parents working so hard to make it a full-time sustainable business. But it was *too much* hard work for both mam and dad, who were now in their fifties.

It was also unprofitable.

So much so that mam had to take a job in a local hosiery factory, whilst dad became the local postman as well as running the nursery. Convenient early hours – early start and early finish – suited him because he could still work the field *after* his morning shift. Eventually, however, this took its toll and we sold up to move back into the village.

I think we lived on the nursery from 1950 to 1954.

I mentioned earlier that we sold the house, land, and business to Estonian refugees. They'd fled a hostile Soviet regime. The daughter of the family was about my age. I vaguely remember her. I learned later that, whilst she remembers those times, she got the actual facts wrong in an article in The Leicester Mercury *saying that her parents had started the nursery*. Much later she had a son who became a politician.

All our family members pitched in raising crops and harvesting. These included brassicas, berry fruits, a salad garden, potatoes and other vegetables, peas and beans, as well as keeping poultry for the eggs. We children were usually employed for the "thinning out" of young plants before they matured, and ultimately picking for market. Brussel sprouts were the worst, picked in February using frozen fingers with frost still on the sprouts. Dad also took on students on a day basis at pea-picking time later in the year.

Other employees, albeit casual, included Mr. Toone ("Tooney") and Mr. Paramour. These solid, hard-working, dependable locals were your typical casual agricultural labourers from the village. Both would arrive together by bike, which was a comical scene in a way since Mr. Paramour was about half as tall again as

Tooney. I enjoyed this contact with these honest folk outside of the family, even though they rarely stopped to talk with me and just got on with their work.

David Thomas was different, though, being younger (in his teens?) and, apparently not so hard-working. He was easily distracted by a pestering 5-year-old.

Brian was coming up to school-leaving age by then and could help dad enormously because he drove the tractor – an old Fordson Major. It was old and temperamental and stalled every few minutes. Eventually we found out it was a blocked filter. Brian told me recently that Farmer Rest, in the village, apparently diagnosed this for dad. I loved the tractor, especially when dad let me sit on the back of the harrow for extra weight (!).

All four stone of me.

Another tractor in the lives of Brian and John (me) was a little grey Ferguson owned by Blaby Rose Gardens, run by Dutch people – owner and manager - Mr Beschovel and Mr Hanraads, respectively. Beschovel didn't seem too keen on dad, mainly because he wouldn't sell the land to him. Also dad let some sections go fallow some years and Beschovel didn't like the weeds seeding his rose crops.

But Mr Hanraads was lovely and once let us sit on his tractor while he took a photograph of Brian and me. This I still have. He and his wife stayed friends with us long after we left Hillview Nurseries. I think I'm right in saying that his sons, or at least one of them, carried on in the same business and founded The Leicester

Rose Company. (I think!)

As I said, Brian was about to start work, so his help for dad was limited to evenings and weekends. The job he took was – guess where – at English Electric. Brian had gone to South Wigston Secondary Moderrn school where his best subject seemed to have been Technical Drawing. No surprise then that he was taken on as an Apprentice Draughtsman.

Two things now come to mind.

Sister Betty already worked there - in the office as a shorthand typist (then secretary) and cycled to work on a yellow and black, drop-handle-bar Dawes Domino (I think). So did Brian, at least it was the same make and model but with a cross-bar, probably bought on the new way of buying things you couldn't afford - a new idea from America called hire-purchase.

Unfortunately he got it stolen when he left it outside Sammy Wale's house in The Avenue - whilst they went to the cinema. (The Plaza, in Whetstone, before it closed to become AGM Crisp Factory).

But the bit that tickled me was that that mam went with Brian for his interview at English Electric. I guess he had to have mam there because a minor wasn't allowed to sign an apprenticeship contract. But I still carry with me a vision of my fresh-faced brother sat in front of the foreman at English Electric while my mam told him what a good, conscientious boy he was.

True, I suppose.

Overall I remember those days at Hillview Nurseries with a great deal of fondness, even though no friends from school ever made it the mile or so out of the village to play evenings or weekends. One exception was Adrian ("Age") Meredith who came out *one time* on my birthday. I made him jam sandwiches because my mam was still at work and dad was out in the field.

I know it's a bit late, Adrian, but thank you.

Some things you never forget.

The big event, though, and one I was never *allowed* to forget, was the time I set the Christmas tree on fire! The family never let me forget it.

Later, as a teenager I rarely took a girl home but, if ever I did, I was always reminded – usually by my sister Joan telling them: "Did he tell you he set the Christmas tree on fire?".

I mean, as if I would. How embarrassing.

Anyway, here's what happened.

Dad and Brian were working in the field. At that time it got dark about 4 o'clock. I'd been reading a comic showing a tree decorated with candles. Ours was decked in cotton wool. It looked so lame in comparison so I must have decided to do something about it. The open fire was roaring away in the lounge on the chilly December afternoon. I folded up some newspaper, lit it, and put the taper to one of the pieces of cotton wool.

Woosh! It all flared up, clearly out of control within seconds. I had no idea how to put it out and I was on my own in the house, apart from Bess.

Terrified, I opened up the French doors and ran outside shouting, in the direction I guessed Brian and dad were working, "The Christmas tree's on fire! The

Christmas tree's on fire!". They could probably see the flames, even from where they were in the fields.

Dad and Brian ran up to the house.

I ran off to hide in the cabbage field.

Bess followed me.

(Tail wagging! But what was so funny?)

I waited there in the December chill without a coat for what seemed hours, huddled to Bess for warmth. Dark descended but neither dad nor Brian came to look for me. At least I could see there were no longer any flames, we still had a house, and it was still intact. But I was frightened to death of dad's temper. He could flare up even if I did something that was, in my eyes, hardly wrong at all. Just irritating.

But this was serious.

It must have been an hour before I picked out the dark shape of mam - silhouetted against some car headlights - walking up from the village, up the long drive from the main road leading to our house, as she made her way home from work. I called out.

What she must have thought?

I ran across the field to her but Bess beat me to it, greeting mam with tail wagging and, if she were able to talk, probably bursting to tell her what I'd been up to. But that was up to me. I explained to mam what had happened and, of course, that "I didn't mean it". We soon reached the house and she went inside ahead of me as we entered the warmth of the kitchen.

Brian and dad were waiting for me.

Usually, dad would "give me a clout" if I'd

misbehaved - "boxing my ears" as they would say. This time he didn't. He was surprisingly calm. Boy was I relieved. But perhaps there was relief on his part that the damage to the front room was only superficial, needing just fresh wallpaper and a lick of paint to put it right again.

But there was *one* punishment.

Even today, thinking about it, I find it amusing. In those days everyone had a local newspaper delivered - in our case The Leicester Mercury. It ran a comic strip that I followed every day – Ronnie Raindrop. My punishment was that I was not allowed to read Ronnie Raindrop for the next few days. Amazingly light punishment. Dad never laid a finger on me that time. I could hardly believe it. I guess being repeatedly reminded of what I'd done as a child, for the next twenty years or so, was enough. Or worse.

Who says the punishment doesn't fit the crime?

Anyway, with that out of the way can we please get on with the real issues at hand? For instance, there's one thing I just cannot understand even to this day.

I said earlier that Hillview Nurseries was a mile or so out of the village and from where my school was situated in Church Street. That was before the Fairway Estate was built, on which the modern Stokes Primary School was introduced and the old stone-built village school subsequently closed and converted into flats.

Occasionally, in the early days when I was still six or seven years old, dad would take me to school on the cross-bar of his bicycle - his government issue Post Office delivery bike. It was quite painful on my backside, despite the cushion dad tied to the cross-bar. Otherwise, I would have had to walk - as I eventually had to on my own later, as an 8 year-old, along the pavement of the busy Lutterworth Road way out in the country. We seemed quite remote.

The ridiculous part of it all was that I used to go home for lunch, rather than take sandwiches or have school dinners. *I had to make it home and back in one hour.* By special arrangement I was allowed to leave five minutes before the other children. Amazing, looking back on it, taking so much trouble because I wouldn't stay for school dinners - maybe because I was only used to having meals with my own family.

I must have run all the way, there and back.

Before leaving this era and my life as a country boy, I must say something about other experiences that left an indelible, often fond, impression with me.

Such as...

Although the nursery was a smallholding in more ways than one, dad still managed to lay part of it to hay. Without machinery to do the work, dad scythed the grass *by hand*, and made a couple of haystacks, rather than bales. Small ones, granted, but the smell of newly stacked hay was a delight, as was the heat that exuded from them as you burrowed a hole into their centre, large enough to slip both feet inside. In retrospect, I think this heat needed to be released anyway to stop it catching fire spontaneously.

But why did he need hay?

We had no cattle or horses so the only thing I can guess he needed hay for was the chickens. I recall we lost them a time or two, to foxes, all dead in the morning, often with most of their heads bitten off, left for dead. I also recall being fascinated by the so-called 'day-old chicks - little hatchlings milling around in a wire netting enclosure. Of course, there was also the chicken feed that we kept in the house, in the kitchen, warm and dry and away from vermin.

Will I ever forget that smell of chicken feed?

We ate the eggs, obviously, and on special occasions - like Christmas - we would eat one of the chickens. Now *a roast chicken dinner* was a treat at that time, usually preserved for Christmas. They were expensive to buy *if you could get them*. This was way before chicken farms; and way before supermarkets. Which is why we favoured rabbit, sometimes trapped, other times bought from the local butcher.

Life on a market garden in the 1950's was hard - and making a living from it even harder - but, for a young boy, it was unique. Who else can look back on the excitement of finding eight partridge eggs on open farmland? (But remind me next time not to cram them into one pocket of my coat and run excitedly across the field to show my dad. The result can be quite messy.)

But, as I've said, it was hard for my folks. I still have a 1952 diary in which dad documented the changing seasonal patterns, from too much rain, to not enough, from too much frost, or unrelenting hot summer days - and detrimental effects these excesses had on the viability of his crops.

It beat him in the end.

Chapter Five - 69, LUTTERWORTH ROAD

In 1954 we moved from Hillview Nurseries to a house built by a local developer, Len Potter. It was a semi-detached three-bedroom house at 69, Lutterworth Road. Len Potter and his family took the other semi-detached, Number 67. Next door on the other side towards Grove Road was the Police House where the village bobby and his family lived.

Mr Madison was the village policeman at the time.

He had a son, a little younger than me, called Roy. We became friends. Together with Len's daughter, Julia Potter, we used to 'hang out' as you would say now, since we were all about the same age. A couple of things I remember about Roy was that he spoke very well (his dad was on the way to higher things in the force, I reckon), and he had to have a glass of milk *every day* which his grandmother always insisted he had, every afternoon.

Milk? Yuch! I felt was it was gross.

One more thing; you were also not allowed to swear in front of the Madisons and, by swear, I mean the innocuous words "bugger" and "sod". The swear words used commonly today, the 'f' words, were not known by children our age, and you never heard them spoken by parents or any other adult now I come to think of it.

Our bungalow at Hillview Nurseries had been built specially for us, and was detached. I think the semi-detached house on Lutterworth Road cost £1,200. I know mam and dad took out a mortgage for it because occasionally I would Pay our monthly payment into the Leicester Building Society. Clearly, dad saw very little surplus money from the sale of the nursery, but we were able to afford a car - a small Standard 8. Mam still worked in a factory in the village; dad took a job in the stores at the Midland Hosiery Mills in Aylestone.

This may have been quite a step down for him. He would have been over-qualified. I haven't got a CV for him but he may have gone from factory foreman at a young age then, for some reason, left the industry to buy Grove Road Stores - but I'm not sure what year. Perhaps before WW2. They sold that and he became a commercial traveller for Singer before, at some stage, he switched again to become a horticulturalist, buying ten acres of land opposite The Blaby Rose Gardens. It was a quarter of a mile from The Dog and Gun pub and the British Road Services depot.

Quite a career journey, looking back.

As a young man starting out he'd been one of the youngest factory foremen at Percival's in the shoe industry. Dad always maintained an interest in shoes. He sometimes mended his own soles and heals. I still have the last he used to work on. If we bought a pair of new shoes ourselves, we always showed them to dad when we got home for "quality control" inspection.

Anyway, we ended up back in Blaby village in 1954, in a newly-built house, where most of my 'growing-up' years were spent. Events that follow may be somewhat random or, at least, out of chronological order. Broadly, though, they cover my life from age 8 to 11 years old.

The biggest change for me when we sold the nursery was that now I lived in the centre of the village. I had friends, neighbours' children as well as school friends who I would see to play with out of school.

Melvyn Wale was my first long-standing playmate from aged five or six and, although we now live some 180 miles away from each other, over 70 years have passed and we still talk to each other on the phone, every week or so. We both shared friends who we grew up with together – some lasting well into our teens.

Blaby was a rural village then, with open countryside never far away. That led to popular games like "exploring" - usually in the fields and hedgerows nearby where we would construct a base - a den made from branches, planks and anything else we could find. Scrumping was our only venture into crime (stealing apples from local orchards), but mostly we played cowboys and Indians and, pretty soon, soccer overtook all of these activities. This was our 'PG' period.

No, not 'Parental Guidance', but 'Pre-Girls'.

Melvyn became a very successful local soccer player, scoring hundreds of goals over a long period playing for some 40 years. Initially, though he may not remember this or perhaps he'll deny it, he didn't get the hang of the game. He did more damage *to other players* than to the ball. As an 8 year old that earned him the nick-name "kick-'oss Wale".

Cruel though that may seem, and I'm not trying to be mean mentioning it, the name could well have been the making of him. In fact, it may have defined his success. He changed and, for all the years to come, he became a renowned local sportsman (principally soccer and cricket, but also tennis).

Despite his early nick-name, he didn't play dirty.

In addition to sports, he excelled in musical performance as lead singer for the Seven Seas band, then later became an award winner in local drama as both actor and director. But most of all he excelled as a perfect role model and father for his and Sue's delightful children and grandchildren.

Underpinning all this was a solid career as a concrete salesman (no pun intended) and, in the few years prior to retirement after leaving the cement business, a "pied-piper" style sports teacher for the local junior school. This was matched by commendable leadership qualities applied to adult sports management – especially in local soccer.

The main point I am making here is that self-belief can break down so many barriers and allow success to break through, even overturning early set-backs in childhood. But allow me now, dear reader, to fast-forward a few years to my own achievements on the sports field whilst at school.

They were very few.

Only recently have some of "the reasons why" emerged. When we started out on the soccer trail, at ten years old, Melv and I were both spotted by some of the "big kids" in the village for their local soccer team on the park. Big kids is defined by them being 14 years old. One boy in particular inspired me and presented me with my first pair of soccer boots. They were old-style "Tom Finney type" - pure leather with high ankles and studs fixed with nails into the sole. The significance of this is, as the studs wore down, the nails burst through the insole to spike the soles of your feet.

Painful!

I was shoe size 5 and the boots in question were size 7 – but I loved them to bits. Pre-worn as they were, I cleaned and applied dubbin after every match, until we were able to afford a pair of 'continental-style' Adidas boots. They were made popular by the likes of Ferenc Puskas of the game-changing (literally) Hungarian national side, and pioneered by other foreign teams.

That early boost to my confidence led me to be picked for the junior school team, playing on the right wing. I was about ten years old, "OK" as a player (not brilliant) but I was an ever-present, and scored four goals! Mr. Buxton was our form teacher and soccer coach. Derek Pawley was our best player.

The year before that the star was Alan Churchard. Later he emigrated and went on to be a leading national coach in Canada. His talent was unfairly overlooked by professional sides, including Leicester City. But he was a legend to us, as were other school-level players from other teams, such as Nigel (Nidge) Austin and Henry Greasley. How great it must have been, if they had known, to be so admired by your peers when you were not even out of short trousers!

Sycamore Street at the bottom of Cross Street
A feature of the Village Centre - lost

There was an open brook running through the village, parallel to Lutterworth Road. It was just in front of the British Legion and the fish and chip shop at the bottom of cross Street. Blaby Hall, diagonally opposite, bordered on Church Street and Sycamore Street protected by a high brick wall, but against which floodwaters would lap after heavy rainfall, or if the Soar Valley in general was flooded.

We never went into the grounds of Blaby Hall when we were mere junior school kids. 'Enter at your peril' we used to say, if we lost a ball over.

Located down from the cross roads, down Cross Street, you would be pretty much in the epi-centre of the village, given that within a couple of minutes, give or take, you were in reach of: the church - the school - the post office - Barber Lowe and Barber Law - The Baker's Arms - The Black Horse - The George - The Bull's Head as well as The British Legion (wow! five pubs) - a Jet garage - a farrier (back in the day, before my time) - Roberts' newsagent - the Co-op - Meredith's the fishmonger - a butcher - Worthington's the grocer and Johnny Atkins the greengrocer - Mr Bellamy the cobbler... and Pratt Brothers' electrical shop, where you could by home appliances but, most importantly for my age, record players and the latest 45 RPM vinyl records.

Now that's what you call a village!

Chapter Six - SECONDARY SCHOOL

After junior school came secondary school at age 11: South Wigston Boys' High School. It was the same school that my brother had been to some three years earlier when it was a secondary modern school. I'd not passed my 11+ with high enough marks to go straight into Guthlaxton Grammar School and I also narrowly missed a scholarship to Loughborough Art College.

No matter. I loathed the idea of boarding school.

I excelled in what, effectively, was a "lower league" than grammar school academically, being placed in the top class every year, and achieving top pupil in the whole year overall for three straight years.

Sports-wise - not so good, unlike Mick Charlton.

I did make the rugby team in the first year, however, after showing suitable aggression in the gym early on. But in years two and three all the other boys in the team grew; apart from me.

So I was dropped.

I was too small and puny, with little skill at rugby.

The High School was a traditional rugby school of some pedigree; we were not allowed to play soccer on sports day, it was frowned upon; the Grammar School had both rugby and soccer teams. A previous rugby star at South Wigston was Dave Hillsdon, a distant cousin of mine who, as a youngster had been sickly and in very poor health, but who later played for England Youth International. His picture hung in the corridor, proud for all to see. He was later over-looked by

Leicester Tigers due, or so I was told, to some heart condition, although he had a long stint with South Wigston Old Boys rugby club, playing alongside my pal Mick Charlton, as well as Johnny Hallam, Pete Miller, Roger Glover, Roy Weston and other locals.

Out of school, in games with friends from the village on the local park and later at our adopted Westleigh sports ground, I was regarded as a reasonably good player. However, as far as the school team at Guthlaxton was concerned, I was nowhere. I simply didn't make the squad, even as reserve. Sure, it was a much bigger school, but it really didn't make sense. I was *so* disappointed.

Even though I didn't make the team, I was always a loyal supporter and turned up to cheer on our school team. That's when I noticed why I stood out against the rest, and what was holding me back from being picked.

Class discrimination.

They - those who played for the team - all wore Terylene trousers; you know, the quality ones that kept their shape even in the rain. *Mine*, on the other hand, were the cheap wool mix that needed to be ironed every day! Also, on balance, I sensed that their mams didn't work for a living, and that their families were able to exist on the wage of the father. Ha! They were verging on being middle class! Their dads worked in offices rather than factories, like mine.

This was quite openly apparent and the sports teachers doubtless took note when it came to team selection. A veritable clique of regular team members emerged, the elite, loosely based on class, although I guess the school demographic in this solid Labour Party area was upper-working class at best.

Gosh! My first taste of institutional discrimination.

In my later years at the school my parents *were* able to afford Terylene trousers for me, but the dye was already cast and I never made the school soccer team. Just to double the irony, on leaving school, the first soccer team I was invited to join and play for – week-in, week-out – was made up largely of guys from another grammar school who were what I would normally regard as quite posh and from well-off backgrounds, and dads in 'the professions'. Long live meritocracy! My faith in my soccer playing abilities was therefore restored.

At least in the adult game.

I mentioned Dave Freeman earlier. He, together with his mam, two elder brothers and a sister, lived opposite us in The Avenue, Blaby back in the 1940's. Before Melvyn, *he* was my first friend – pre-school and we "palled out" (as we used to say = 'became pals') until his artistic creativity, and my relative lack of it, led to a parting of the ways.

His man must have been divorced, because I never remember seeing a father. Both brothers were also talented artists – commercial artists they were called – before the term 'graphic designer' took over.

Dave was equally talented as his brothers.

That's why and when Dave, Mick Charlton, and I were selected to sit a one-day practical art examination at Loughborough Art College. We travelled to the college some distance away, where I recall we sat to eat "school dinners" served up in a refectory (canteen). This phased me somewhat because I was used to eating sandwiches that I took to school every day when I was at Blaby. The idea of formal dining phased me.

The second thing that made me apprehensive was the prospect of going to a boarding school. I couldn't even contemplate not going home at the end of school every day to the family home and my mam and dad.

I failed the entrance exam – which must have been a big relief. Mick also failed but Dave passed. Actually I'm not sure, but Josephine Shepherd in our year at Blaby Juniors may have also sat the exam and passed. I was always in the top five at junior school and I think Dave and Josephine – plus Lois (Lulu) Bailey – ranked ahead of me, at fourth, with Mick coming in at fifth.

I have no idea why I remember all this.

I saw no more of Dave after age eleven, not even at weekends or school holidays. It must have been my first experience of 'moving on'. Ultimately he went to Canada with his family. I would love to connect with him one final time, though.

Dave? Are you out there?

He was a big guy even then. Nobody started a fight with Dave, although another superb pupil and sportsman – Derek (Dec) Pawley was often compared with him and might have been a match. Nobody was a better fighter than Dec. He was a nice bloke and, thank goodness he was so friendly, as well as being an excellent soccer player. If you're out there as well, Derek, I do hope life has been good to you.

As for Dave, he must have been handsome looking, I guess. I say this because, even at eleven, he had a girlfriend, Pat Jones. I remember she was nuts about Dave. I think I must have wanted a girlfriend too. One particular girl - Lulu Bailey was her name - and best friend of Josephine Shepherd. Jo was nice, but Lulu was rather aloof. Lulu was quite posh whilst I was a tad below her pay grade. I recall that she would never dance with me in country dancing classes. However, another Bailey – Pat, but no relation, did.

Now she *was* an excellent dancer.

If *you*'re still out there, too, Lulu – I hope you had a good life! (With no regrets? Ha!)

The idea of first going to the High School for three years, then to the Grammar School, was pioneered in Leicestershire and called 'The L-Plan'.

It was the prototype Comprehensive System.

Here was the deal: the "Leicestershire Plan" meant you all went to a High School direct from Junior School at 11 years old - irrespective of your educational standard or capabilities. After three years at High School you *had the option* to stay at High School for a further two years – before leaving at aged 15 to go to work. There was no exit examination.

Alternatively - again, irrespective of how intelligent you were - you could elect to go to a Grammar School at aged 13/14. There you would be expected to stay until aged 16 or 17 – another three years. You could then take "Ordinary Level" General Certificates of Education ("G.C.E.'s"), after which, if grades were good enough, you took "Advanced Level" G.C.E.'s.

You needed A-Levels to get into university.

Unlike now, decent A-Level Grades for three subjects - yes, just three - was good enough to be accepted, and it was up to each individual university to set those grades, usually after an interview with the head of the department for your major subject.

Only three subjects you say? When today's scholars take half a dozen or more? But consider this.

Back in the day there were no multiple choice questions so, in my view, the examination process was previously more demanding. Nor were calculators allowed in maths exams. There were fewer universities and the percentage of school leavers going to university was in the region of 3%, whereas nowadays about a half expect to go to university. The lower tier higher education establishments such as polytechnics have, in the main, been upgraded to university status. (Even Huddersfield Technical College to which I was seconded for teaching practice, is now a university.)

I am sure if I were to even suggest that standards have been watered down over the years I might be severely challenged. However, I would be equally put out if there were any suggestion that we were less intelligent some fifty years ago.

The other option to taking full-time formal education and qualifications was to "take articles" in a profession - such as barrister or accountant. Becoming an 'articled clerk' involved *your parents paying* the law firm or accountant practice for your training – I think up to 5 years. For the record – the latter was out of the question for me, although one of my best friends – Mick Charlton – took this route.

Anyway, back to the plot.

I did well at South Wigston Boys' High School, after narrowly missing going to Grammar School at 11 years old because my "11-plus" exam results were not high enough. I was, however, placed into the *top class* (or stream) *at High School*, where I was top *of* the class every year for three years until leaving to go to the *4th Year* at Guthlaxton Grammar School.

My very good friend, Mick Charlton, also made the top class at High School where he was always in second place, for three years. My lifelong friend, Melvyn, was two classes below me. Just saying that for reference. *Not having a go, Melv!*

I made the High School team in rugby and cricket – but I knew I was an after-thought for the latter, just to make up the numbers, whereas Mick was a real star at both. A superb athlete.

The other transformation occurred in athletics. At junior school I usually came 3rd to Dave Freeman's 1st and Derek Pawley's 2nd at the 100 yard sprint. Mick always came 4th. Then, at High School, Mick could suddenly out-run me – essential for his rugby – and he was a brilliant all-rounder at cricket - an excellent fast bowler as well as batsman.

Latterly, I was positioned - or should I say relegated

to - full-back at rugby, or "lost" in the scrum. Likewise. at cricket I was always last to bat and placed on the boundary when fielding but – most importantly, I was delegated (relegated again?) as scorer or 12th-man.

A "Nobody".

I hated both roles in both sports. I hated being an also-ran. Rugby meant cycling to school in sub-zero temperatures on Saturday morning in mid-winter – to play in freezing cold on a frost-baked muddy pitch, just to make up the numbers. Worse still, cricket involved staying after school lessons finished - until 6 o'clock in the evening - and being late for tea. Both sucked. Even a school trip to Twickenham – I guess to see the England international rugby team play and a free trip to Leicester Tigers rugby ground - meant very little to me.

(I recall the Tigers' ground was in such a sorry state, the wooden stands – the steps – were so rotten as to be unsafe. Compare that to now.)

The High School building was divided into two blocks with two separate entrances – one for girls, the other for boys. To clarify, the actual building, classrooms *and staff* were divided into two separately run schools. Layout-wise, imagine a semi-detached house where each half is a mirror image, in reverse, of the other. The only time we were able to mix with the girls was at break, on the grass playing fields. For the first two years we tended to keep ourselves separate – using free time to play soccer in the playground. Boys mixing with boys, girls with girls. But later on, as we were maturing you might say, 'becoming more aware', there was an increased level of interaction. The usual – pretty innocent – stuff with girls was a new experience for some of us, behind the bike sheds.

No touching. Well, not much, anyway.

Once in the Third Year, as teenagers, we switched our attention much more fully to girls. Some more fully than others. They were exciting times although I never formed any close attachments – unlike Mick who, at a seemingly early age, "went steady" with Mary Featherby. Various of my other school friends had girlfriends – on and off.

About that time, but nothing to do with what I've just been talking about, I noticed a lad who was later to become 'one of our Blaby circle' and fellow soccer team-mate - Steve Jarvis. For some reason he stood out from the rest of the kids - primarily due to how good he was at sports. He was a year below me so this was only at break-time. It was not until I was 20 years old that he moved to our village from Wigston. He soon integrated into our group in the village, because he was good fun and shred our passion for soccer. He was also in a band with one of our crowd - Ken - so it was only natural he should be included and naturally became friends on and off the soccer field.

He was still an excellent player.

But what I didn't know in those days before he moved to the village, before I actually knew him, was that then, as a 13-year-old, he used to go out with a girl with whom I later became totally captivated.

To save her blushes, I will call her Dark Eyes.

I never spoke to Steve about this – not even all those years later when we'd become close friends. Sadly, he has since died, but by that time our friendship had become "disconnected" by geography and not replaced by technology. Having left home in 1970 to move permanently to Devon there was no contact - there were no mobile phones, no internet. It wasn't until years later that I was so pleased to meet up with him one final time at a reunion – 47 years later!

Ironically, I learnt then that he'd since started to see Dark Eyes again when he was in his sixties – only a few years before he died. Even though he'd gone out with the girl who, at the time as a teenager, had been the girl of my dreams, I never begrudged him that privilege and he never knew how I'd felt about her. I always saw him as a dear friend, admittedly with just a touch of envy – even though he'd won the heart of the girl I'd "loved" as a 16-year-old.

I might as well talk about Dark Eyes now, to lay it all to rest. Romantically I thought of nobody else, pretty much, for six or seven years. I declared how I felt about her in a brief letter I handed to her one day when she was walking home from school with her sister. They'd just cut through from Park Road to the Dovedale Avenue and Queens Road area before joining The Fairway where they lived.

She replied some days later with a letter, delivered in similar fashion, by hand. I kept it for some eight years, carrying it in my wallet wherever I went, before I finally burnt it in the hope of destroying the memory. In her letter she explained that she couldn't go out with me and that there were "other fish in the sea" beside her. (Her words.)

There weren't, not until years later.

For those interim years I suffered in silence. I never contacted or bothered her again. I guess that was to my credit. One hears so many instances these days when the kind of fixation I suffered leads to "stalking". Thankfully I never descended into that, which must have been so difficult for me because she lived close by in the same village. Not only that, she was clearly "the village beauty" and her name came up many, many times as a random, casual mention among friends – especially by those who were in her class at school.

Although I was a 'normal' teenager, I can hardly call it a fascination driven by sex. I had always been a hopeless romantic when it came to "the ideal girl" - enthralled by film-stars such as Sophia Loren, Nathalie Wood and Doris Day.

All I wanted was to lay down in the tall grass on a warm summer's day, looking up at the shapes of the clouds in a clear blue sky with the girl of my dreams next to me. With my faithful dog, Bess, of course. Barely talking. Doing no more than holding hands.

(No! Not with the dawg! With Dark Eyes.)

I guess she went to university far away for most of the time for which I was "carrying this torch", and before I left Blaby. But the rejection she handed me when I was a 16-year-old until my early twenties shaped my personality, my moods, my relationships with close friends and family. Most of all it became a barrier to my accepting any other girl as a substitute. It was amazing I managed to keep so many friends – or indeed any! I was such a pain most of the time. Don't get me wrong – I did have the occasional girlfriend – but they were half-hearted relationships and never went anywhere.

Anyway. More of this, later.

I suffered at Grammar School compared with High School. The Dark Eyes episode was a constant cloud hanging over me and it had clearly knocked my self-confidence. Academically I performed poorly in class. I was so used to being 1st in exams and class work at High School, but at Guthlaxton I averaged 13th - half-way down the rankings. Mick (Charlton) over-took me – coming in at 6th or thereabouts. Furthermore, he excelled even more at rugby and cricket. Again, I never begrudged him that - he deserved it, and we still talk occasionally over the phone. He's still in Leicester, I'm in Devon. He's one of those rarities, someone who never seems to have a bad word said against him whenever his name is mentioned.

What *was* to my advantage, or so I'd hoped when I first went to Guthlaxton, there was a soccer option, whereas South Wigston Boys' High was purely a rugby school. However, I failed to shine in practice and trials, so I never made the team.

Things were not looking too bright!

Why *were* lessons *so* difficult? I always had my doubts and insecurities at High School and never took my 1st place for granted; but 13th? I found myself in another league and couldn't cut it!

I just wasn't good enough.

All this time the Dark Eyes shadow haunted me day-by-day, month-in-month-out, during my most important school years. OK, so it wasn't all bad. I made new friends in class – different friends from those in the village, out of school. So I had two sets of friends – with sport being at the centre. The "girls thing" at school was something I had to get used to – something new, compared with the all-boys High School.

Naturally I gravitated towards, and seemed to get on with, girls who were considered attractive. On the one hand that was fun, but on the other I couldn't shake off my issues with Dark Eyes and find someone as a girlfriend, or just a simple friend. This didn't help when Dark Eyes – in a year below – started at the same Grammar School.

So near yet …

My first proper kiss with any girl came at 14-years-old, at Jane Thomas' party, but not with Jane herself. She was platinum blonde, with bright red lips, a bubbly personality, but not one to whom I would be attracted. The Dark Eyes 'thing' always got in the way in any case. Her best friend was Diane Pearson – another blonde – who we *all* loved as a lovely fun girl, but one who knew how to keep us all at the right distance, romance-wise.

She was THE most popular girl in my year, for the right reasons. She was a good person. Best of all, she never traded on her popularity or looked down on the rest of us, or other girls in school. She had class and you respected that.

I do hope things in life turned out well for her.

Meanwhile, back at Jane Thomas' party. I cannot remember the *name* of the girl I first *kissed*, but I do remember that she had a withered leg – perhaps due to polio? I don't bring that up out of disrespect or to embarrass. In fact, she was really pretty.

So how did that first kiss come about?

At the party we had "Postman's Knock", where one girl and one boy would be picked out of a hat at random to go off – in this case into the under-stairs cupboard - and kiss. (Snog!) That girl and I only ever kissed that one time; and we never talked to each other – before, during or since.

The only other aspect I recall from the night of that party – front of mind as I was actually cycling over to it – were the news reports coming over the radio just before I set out from home. They were about race riots in Little Rock. I had no idea where Little Rock, Arkansas was, but I had this irrational notion - fear almost - that "*they* were coming over here" to cause trouble. Ridiculous. Why? And who were 'they'?

Fellow class-mates I mixed with – boys and girls – gave me an OK social life despite my hang-ups. That said, maybe I should have studied harder IN CLASS and have been more disciplined. As a result, my G.C.E. O-Levels were mediocre and I barely qualified for A-Levels in Six Form.

I was hardly a good candidate for university.

The crowd I mixed with in the first term at 6th Form were not doing me any good. Not that they were a bad influence individually, but we spent a lot of time on an open recreational area called the 6th Form Landing – our "territory". It was there we did the *minimum* of A-Level study, and the *maximum* talking, messing about, and playing our guitars. There was little supervision and I guess this just highlighted our immaturity, lack of discipline, but also a lack of mentoring from teachers.

After three months studying A-Levels I left without further qualifications apart from five O-Levels, at Christmas, to look for work. My dad wanted me to be a barrister, or sign up for a career in the RAF or police force. In the end I got a job as an insurance clerk with a January 1963 start.

Dad was OK about that because it was 'almost' a profession, similar to accountants and solicitors.

Almost.

A typical village feature
The Ford, off Mill Lane, on the River Sence

This was one of our favourite places.

When we began secondary school in Wigston, we'd take the Jitty home, across open fields on foot or cycling. It took us to the Ford. Now, or so I'm told, the trout are back in the River Sence, whereas they'd all disappeared at one stage.

It must have been polluted in those days.

The Jitty takes you across fields to the back of the village - to Wigston Road and Church Street - but, if you cross over The Ford you find Mill Lane. Readers of my novel, 'Finding Rose', will recognise it as the location of a Romani camp - which it was, off and on.

If the Soar Valley flooded - which was often - the river overflowed into fields bordering The Ford, making them virtually impassible despite an elevated causeway stretching across and dividing the grazing land into two meadows.

I mentioned Wigston Road. On or around that area was Doctor Drury's surgery. He did house calls then! Following the road round you would arrive at the centuries old 'Bakers Arms' where, back in the day, for a ha'penny (Google that one!) you could ask for your home-made loaves to be baked.

Next to 'The Bakers' is the village green - 'Greenie' - but it was tarmac the last I looked.

Shame.

This is old Blaby where, at the time I was at Junior School nearby, cottages there were under threat of being torn down due to health risks. They must have been renovated and reprieved I guess.

Chapter Seven - I START WORK

As I said, insurance was considered an "almost" profession and not the same as an accountant, solicitor or barrister. Or officer in the military. Ironically, the one characteristic that *did* provide some degree of credibility and status within insurance was the presence of ex-military officers in management.

That was then. Things are different now.

For a junior clerk in the midst of this aspiring elite commercial environment it helped me develop *some* degree of professionalism in terms of bearing, dress and respect. Looking back, it was so cool to be addressed as "old boy" by a retired colonel or ex-RAF officer, and a privilege to be asked to run errands for cigarettes. Better still to be "tipped" with a couple of premium Peter Stuyvesant! (Above my pay grade.)

Unlike modern insurance providers based largely on brand-building marketing – companies in the '60's had their roots in tradition and were founded during the industrial revolution two centuries earlier.

What was that like?

You have to imagine a work ethic not based on modern technology. There was no internet, no mobile phone networks, no computer base of any kind. It was all paper, typewriters, land phones, hand-written record cards and face-to-face contact.

These days, email provides immediacy; then, the equivalent – at least in cities like Leicester – were four mail collections and deliveries PER DAY. I repeat: FOUR collections and deliveries. On top of that, and perhaps to save money on postage stamps, one of my tasks was to *hand-deliver* post to brokers, legal firms and other insurance companies in the city centre.

Looking back, that was so funny. Weird, in fact. I had licence to "take a walk" for an hour around the city – or for however long deliveries lasted – dropping off documents and picking up sandwiches for colleagues.

To cap it all, that year – early 1963 – was "the big freeze". Snow hit – February?- and icy pavements lasted into April! But did I care? Apart from the "why did you take so long, John?" reprimand from the Chief Clerk, Mr. Hemingwray, on my return; no.

Life so far had been very much village based, but I was not phased by life in the city. Nor was my best friend Melvyn, who worked in retail - at Dunn and Company, Gentleman's Outfitters - and later in shoe manufacturing as a foreman.

We met up regularly at lunchtimes. This included a Friday treat now and again at the exotic – for us – Hung Lau Chinese restaurant. It cost four shillings – real extravagance. Twenty pence (cents) at today's money, but we did only earn seven pounds a week. Recently I learnt that Hung Lau was run by the father of TV celebrity chef, Gok Wan!

By this time, we – Melvyn and I – had started to go out at weekends to dances. They were dance-halls, since there were no discos or clubs as we know now. Occasionally – on a Friday – we also went to the Palais de Dance for a *lunch-hour* of dancing to records.

It was an early version of disco.

It cost a shilling. (Five pence)

Of course, our main aim was to meet girls. I still had my hang-up over "you know who" and Melvyn did have casual girlfriends but he'd still yet to meet "the right one". Just to demonstrate what a sad person I was, there was a girl in the typing pool who was pestering me to go out with her.

I had no interest.

Later in the year we re-located to Charles Street when we merged with another The Commercial Union – only to attract yet another girl to spend most of the day making eyes at me from across the office. *Two of them.* In competition! I am not showing off or anything. Really. I'm not. It's just to say what a hopeless case I was right then.

The merger with the North British and Mercantile Insurance Company (how traditional is that!) brought changes. I took on more responsibility. We were a fun group of work colleagues at this new, larger office. However, with promotion came the requirement to take professional exams. I tried to study but my heart just wasn't in it. I was bored by the prospect. So I resigned.

But just before I resigned...I was in a good place.

I was at a stage of quite enjoying life in Leicester – at least at lunch-hours. As well as Chinese cuisine and mid-day dance hour on Fridays we had a strong coffee-bar culture. Since relocating offices, so had Melvyn, changing from a career in retail into manufacturing. We found we were virtually next-door neighbours, at the far end of Charles Street.

We were able to add snooker and darts into our lunch-hour recreation, including a couple of pints of Everards finest beer in nearby pubs as well as packing into a local coffee-bar to ring the changes. There we kept the jukebox fuelled with sixpences (sorry, Google that, too), keeping ourselves filled with expresso coffee and toasted teacakes lathered in butter.

Heaven!

It was so much fun. We all had jobs and enough money to spend. Rock and roll was bursting onto the scene. We were teenagers for goodness sake.

What's not to like?

I should say at this point that soccer was a massive part of all this – not just *watching* Leicester City but also forming and playing for a local team in a local league in which Melvyn and I were team-mates.

Outside of work, and with no girl-friend, soccer became a major focus of my life.

And music.

Music was probably equal first along with soccer when it came to our consuming interest - at sixteen years old.

By October 1962 we were already well into The Beatles and the Mersey Sound - The Big Three, The Hollies, Gerry and the Pacemakers - plus a remaining obsession with American groups. We had also begun to notice a fellow called Bob Dylan. In fact, our first song performed at the church concert was 'Blowing in the Wind'. But, hang on a minute.

Who are we talking about? Who are 'we'.

We are - or were - The Denhams. Initially Melv and me, on guitars and vocals. This was quickly followed by two more additions - two sets of two, actually. Girls. My cousin Shirley plus her friend Elaine. Harmonising. I can still hear their rendition of 'I'll Get You' taken from a Beatles album. And then there were Carol Elgar and Susan Hackney - performing as a duo quite separately from Shirley and Elaine - again harmonising. I think their main number was 'You Don't Have To Be A Baby To Cry'.

So, there were six of us - three sets of two - but we never sang as a group of six. Why was that?

For some reason, the girls dropped out. Not sure why, but it was nothing to do with the fact that Melv 'dated', I guess you would call it, Shirley, Carol and Susan - previously - *and not all at the same time!*

The re-formed Denhams became Melv and me, plus Mick Giles on bass guitar and Phil Gibson ('Gibbo') until he left for university and was replaced by a drummer from the Eyres Monsell.

Before I forget, there was a fifth 'Denham' - Melv's mother, the wonderful Mrs Wale. Not only did she find us gigs, she also drove us to them, as well as recording the only evidence we actually existed - songs taken from our rehearsal in a local village hall, captured on a reel-to-reel Phillips tape recorder.

Melv and I listened to it a couple of years ago, and we weren't too bad - allowing for poor recording equipment and 'undeveloped' musicianship. And, the most amazing part of it all was that our song list covered thirty numbers, including a couple we penned ourselves. I mention this because, after a fifty year gap I began to sing and play again, and in a local groups here in Devon, but with the assistance of chords and lyrics. Back in the day, we memorised every word.

Sadly, after only a few months - a couple of years at the most - we split up. We argued, but don't ask me what it was all about. Ego's, I guess. I packed it all in, whilst Melv went on to be lead singer for The Seven Seas, a very accomplished group, as was Melv.

Ironically, his time with them was cut short. Why? It was a soccer injury - and a cartilage operation - which meant he had to keep off is feet, so the band took on a replacement lead singer.

On the positive side, Melv and I are still best of friends, keeping in touch by phone virtually every week. And neither of us can remember how or why we actually broke up The Denhams.

Melv started a family around this point, whilst Phil and Mick went off to university. That's where my focus switched, as long as I could pass my A-Levels.

Chapter Eight -
GOODBYE INSURANCE - HELLO...?

My plan was to gain two A-Levels and apply for university to read English. Our friend, Phil, was already at Newcastle University and I was inspired by his stories of university life. I signed up for Latin, English and Spanish at A-Level at The Charles Keene College of Further Education for two years, in 1965. If I got the promise of a place and achieved my grades, I would also go to Newcastle University, given the chance. And the grades.

I had a plan (at last!) and, in a way, this was funded by my brother-in-law Derek – my sister's husband and "second dad". He set me up as a self-employed window-cleaner which enabled me to work 20 hours a week, earn as much as I had full-time in insurance, whilst releasing me for 15 hours attendance at college.

Perfect! (Thank you, Derek.)

After initial fear of heights I mastered this craft and earned an excellent hourly rate – necessary, of course, to compensate for bad weather. At least I could use any down-time effectively, in study. I also became extremely fit and agile, with not an ounce of fat on me. However, there were some derogatory remarks from my peers regarding the *status* of my employment. Being a window cleaner was considered very low grade – worthy only of those who didn't have the ability or imagination to do anything else. That said, I was earning more than most of them in half the time.

My parents were OK with my new career path and comfortable with me being a window cleaner. After all, their son-in-law Derek was making good money as such, and providing a good life for his family. The only funny thing was, Derek didn't understand why I needed all that education when I could have earned twice as much by doing twice as many hours. If I wanted to. I was thinking much longer term. The satisfaction of "working my way through college" to better myself was enough – and counteracted any prejudice against the means by which I was achieving my goals.

Because fellow students were also in the 19 to 20 age range I fitted in well. It was not really like going back to school – even though I could have stayed on *at school* two years earlier, for the same qualifications. But this new plan gave me a nice work><study balance. I was earning and I was learning.

Most important, I had an aim in life.

I made new friends in college and, around about the same time, also made new friends out of college but in our village of Blaby. Enter Russ and Ken – who are still friends to this day. They were younger than me and still at Grammar School when we first hooked up together. As it turned out, some of the guys I befriended at college also knew Russ and Ken.

Baz Long was one. The others' names escape me.

Boring though it may be to say this, I was still hung up on Dark Eyes, even though I still managed to go out with one or two girls. They were not serious, didn't last and – apart from one – weren't full relationships, *if you know what I mean*. But there were two girls at college who *were* worth getting to know(!).

One was just like a fashion model and in my class.

Eventually we went out on a date.

It was a disaster.

She had a friend, so I fixed her up with Ken on a blind date to make up the four. Ken is taller than me, but his date even towered over him. Ken hated me for it. I never saw the model again outside of college.

I was pretty clueless handling situations.

What was I thinking? But I wasn't totally useless.

I fared much, much better with the other girl who I will call 'Susan'. It may have actually been her name. She had a younger sister, 'Sally', who went to school with Ken and Russ. For the whole second year, until my course ended, there she was - this beautiful girl ('Susan') - who I would see in the canteen or in the corridor between classes. I think she was studying Commerce. But I can't recall ever actually *talking* to her *at college*. Any communication or connection at all was no more than a look or hint of a smile as we passed each other in the corridor between classes.

That lasted until the end of term.

Back then, the fun part of being in a crowd was 'getting mobile' as The Who song says, piling into someone's car and driving out to some pub in the country, the wonderful East Leicestershire countryside.

The Langtons in summer.

You had to be there to really understand, but it was

magical. Maybe half a dozen or more car loads would descend on one country pub. For the occasion in question it was the end of term get-together for Ken and Russ' year at Guthlaxton Grammar School. It was a warm June or July night – with music and dancing.

I think I must have been given a lift out with Baz Long. Imagine my delight when *who should be there* but 'Susan'. Her sister was there, too, as were Russ (Dallimore, not Lakin) and Ken and a whole bunch of others – I guess Elmo (in his open-top Morris Minor!), Wainy, Nick, Johnny Carter, Stu Gamble – many more.

As the night wore on, with a couple or three pints in me, I asked Susan to dance.

She said "yes".

We danced together - *all night* - until the pub closed. So now I'm thinking, "We're getting on so well. How come I wasted a whole year at college before having the gumption to get to know her properly." As luck would have it, she lived not far from Baz Long. He drove me back home – with Susan and me on the back seat of his car getting to know each other even better. OK, before you ask, "nothing else happened". Not like that, anyway. And I was OK with that - yes, really, but not with what followed.

Nothing.

I never saw her again. I *may* have had her phone number – but somehow we never arranged to meet again. The relationship finished without even starting but I tell you now, *for certain* she would have erased all my sad issues with Dark Eyes. She really was something else and I was so clueless – no, so stupid – that I never even tried to find a way to contact her again. My college courses had finished but, if I had any gumption at all, I might have turned up at Charles Keene CFE just on the off-chance that she might have signed up for another three terms in September.

So it was no joy with Susan, no joy with university acceptance, and back to window-cleaning.

Although I was able to drive, I didn't buy a car until after I left that college. Therefore, when it came to work, I had to ride 4-5 miles carrying my ladder and bucket on my push-bike. Likewise, it was two bus rides and an hour travelling some five miles from home to college, in Leicester. In those days you just did it.

You had to.

As I've said, my A-Level grades were not good enough for me to take up the provisional places reserved at Newcastle University or at the brand new campus at Warwick. I remember the latter so well, because the service roads had just been laid, and there was no grass, just bare earth, in the surrounds. Now I come to think of it, there was one feature of the trip up to Newcastle for my interview I remember well. I bought a copy of the bestselling novel at the time, Catch 22, but couldn't get into it. I've made three attempts since, and still haven't managed more that a few dozen pages.

The end result was - I carried on cleaning windows. I guess I still only averaged 30 hours a week "earning". As you can imagine I didn't mind that. Plus, I was bringing in good money – enough to buy my first car.

A Volkswagen Beetle.

Throughout college I still paid my parents full board for living at home. This was £4.00 a week from a wage of some £10.00 or so. If I earned, say, £12.00 in any week, I would give them double what they asked for. I always seemed to have enough money for what I needed for myself. They deserved it more than I did. They both worked long hours but were not high earners. I was so pleased to make a substantial improvement to their quality of life. It was great to know they were "more comfortable".

Chapter Nine -
ROLL OVER ~~BEETHOVEN~~ VOLKSWAGEN!

I'd learnt to drive with a driving school topped up with lessons from my dad in his Morris Oxford at weekends. On the second test I passed.

That Friday I asked, "Is it OK if I borrow the car?"

The answer was a firm, "No."

Forever. It was fine for me to drive as a learner, with dad in the passenger seat, but not for me to take it out on my own. I was quite taken aback. After all, he'd let Brian take his girlfriend out. But Brian was sensible, of course. Not like me, down the pub every night. But dad was right to refuse me.

I had to buy my own car - a ten year old VW.

I paid £130 for it. A few weeks later I drove it into a ditch one night, coming back from the pub. Luckily there was only minor damage to the car, the ditch survived, and neither I – nor my passenger, Phil – were hurt. Not physically, that is.

But Phil would never ride with me again!

Having a car meant I was more flexible for work, and I could go out at night without having to rely on buses. Just to recap. I failed to get into university so I carried on as a window-cleaner. However, this was only supposed to be a temporary measure whilst I looked for a proper job. Looking back, I was still not *exactly* sure what I wanted, career-wise. That's why it proved harder than I expected.

I do remember being inspired by some close friends who worked for companies selling into the grocery trade – as travelling salesmen. The appeal largely lay in the fact that these jobs came with a brand new car. Usually a Morris 1100. I applied to a few companies, including the biscuit company my friends worked for - as well as to Walkers Crisps. I can still remember that particular one. I was clearly unsuitable for the position and the guy who interviewed me told me to stick to cleaning windows.

Really? Was he serious?

I proved a dismal failure at all the job interviews for which I applied. When questioned, I was unconvincing trying to explain why I wanted the job – given that I was obviously quite intelligent, now with seven O-Levels and two (albeit low-grade) A-Levels - but on the other hand I was happy being a window-cleaner.

Apparently.

Finally, it was on one of these trips to an interview - this time in Trowbridge, an hour or so away – that I miss-judged a bend in Corsham and rolled the VW.

The car was a write-off.

(When I got back home, by bus and train, my dad hardly said anything. I daresay it was enough that he felt he'd made the right decision refusing to let me borrow *his* car.)

The remarkable thing was, immediately after the accident, within the hour, I set out by bus from Corsham to Trowbridge for the interview. My initiative must have impressed them. A few days later I got a letter – from Express Dairies offering me a position – but in Coventry, seventeen miles away from where I lived. The irony of it all. With no car, and no desire to re-locate to Coventry, I turned it down.

Or should I say, 'I wrote it off'?

I went without a car for quite a few months and reverted back to cycling to my window-cleaning round. Although this put me in a social disadvantage as far as being able to get around, by some accident of fortune I was closer to my first "full relationship" with a girl.

OK. How else would you describe it?

But on one occasion, just before I wrote off my car, I was getting on well with this girl we used to see at a pub out at Gumley, or some-such Leicestershire village. They had a band playing at weekends and dancing, so we – a crowd of us from Blaby plus Wainy from Braunstone - made it a regular feature.

Anyway, back to this accident of fortune, we - this girl and I - had arranged to meet up the following Thursday after my Trowbridge episode, to play tennis. That was the pretence, anyway - the last thing on my mind and, I know for certain, the last thing on hers! This was all agreed on the Sunday. My interview – and car crash took place on the Tuesday, two days before. As a result I effectively "stood her up" - but quite unintentionally.

I mean, come on – why would I?

But by the next time I saw her it became clear I'd blown it. We all went out to Gumley the following week, I was a passenger this time, I saw her again and I tried to explain why I was a 'no show'.

Bummer!

She would have none of it. End of... but shortly afterwards I had better luck – if that's the right word.

Paul and I were in Leicester having a drink in some pub or other when it happened. I knew Paul because he'd been in the same class as Russ and Ken, but by now had left school. We were just sat, chatting, when this real beauty of a blonde girl caught my eye. She was with three others – two guys and another girl. I just kept looking over – I couldn't help it until, in the end, she spoke. First. To me.

That was it.

She gave me the nod and I just went over and sat with her, and her three friends, including the guy she was supposed to be with. I ignored him, and the other two, just concentrating on her. At the time, the pop star Lulu had just burst onto the scene. She reminded me of Lulu. Or was it Adrienne Poster? (Google it.) We chatted and, as it turned out he was her blind date, but she was in no way interested.

Enter John-Boy...

I must have still been without a car because I didn't get to take her home, or anywhere else, and we had to meet up at the main bus station on future dates, and so on. We went out a couple or three times during which our attraction progressed to advanced intimacy.

Well, again, what else should I call it?

Finally, when my parents were away on their two week summer holiday (and I was "home alone") we did the deed. That's all I'm going to say about it, mainly because, much to my shame I was rubbish at it on that first occasion. Without trying to rationalise too much, I suppose I was looking for more, more in terms of a closer non-physical relationship alongside the physical one – and we'd hardly even started to connect other than on a physical basis.

We split up soon after.

What I *do* remember on the day "it happened" was that, amusingly, my pal Phil knocked on the door 'whilst I was entertaining', to see if I wanted to go to the pub that evening. He was so put out when I said I was busy and that he couldn't come in. Ha! Without explaining exactly why. Everyone else seemed to be away or busy at that particular time. Russ was in Wales visiting friends and family, Melv - and perhaps Ken - had steady girlfriends or were married, no idea where Jarvo was, nor Paul, nor Wainy, and the 'Davids' (alias Smith and Bell) usually went off on their own into town, so Phil just had to trudge off to the pub on his own.

No matter. It was just funny at the time.

Chapter Ten -
RUSS AND I PLAN OUR ROAD TRIP

I will fast forward 3-4 years now, to when I was about 23 years old. Russ and I set out from our respective homes to "migrate"- down south to Devon and Cornwall. We were tired of the "same-old-same-old" - the reason why we left.

Up to that point, the highlight of the week was always playing soccer for our local team. For me at any rate. The camaraderie in those soccer clubs was exceptional. Unique. The sense of belonging was unequalled but beyond that, as far as I was concerned the rest of the week tended to be uninspiring. The end of each match was like a shutter coming down as the final whistle blew.

Sure, there was a group of us who gathered down the pub at weekends and randomly mid-week. Some of us – but not me – started to get serious 'girl-wise', and this period was interspersed by the odd wedding (!).

Some even started a family.

Others among us began making noises about emigrating to Australia or Canada. Ray Churchard's elder brother had gone there years earlier. Looking back I have to laugh at myself when I recall why I didn't take up any of those £10.00 passages to a New World. In particular I was dead against NZ and Australia because of reports that pubs closed before 9.00 pm.

What!? Nine o'clock?

I was never a heavy drinker, volume-wise, but I was regular. Pub life meant so much to me at the time that it was a deal breaker.

There was no way I was going there!

After a year of "talking about it", Ray and one of the guys, Tony Wainwright (Wainy), emigrated to Canada. The fact that Wainy had just finished with his girlfriend, Gill, was the tipping point for him, whereas Ray just needed to explore other options.

Within our group there was a sub-group as it were – Wainy, Ken and Russ. Russ and I were team-mates as well as pals off the pitch but he was always with some girl or other, whereas I was, well, you know the rest.

Above all, I could never get over the fact that I had so many friends, 'belonged' to a great group of guys - the soccer team - yet I felt so lonely.

The year before Wainy and Ray emigrated we all went down to St. Ives on holiday. Russ, Steve Jarvis (Jarvo) and myself made up the quorum. I don't think Dave Bell went – not sure why. Phil might have started a new life with the BBC in London by then.

Not sure.

Dave Smith was married, as was Melv, and Ken.

I met a girl on that holiday and continued to see her on and off in Liverpool (where she was from) or in St. Ives (where she worked in a hotel). After a while it was apparent that relationship was going nowhere. It must have been because Russ was "between girlfriends" that we finally came to a joint decision. I don't really remember the full circumstances. But the idea of a road trip to the sunny beaches of Cornwall galvanised over the winter, ending with us both quitting our jobs the following spring and setting off in my Wolseley 15/50.

It was April 1970; we each had £100 saved.

Don't ask me why, but at no point did I have any doubts that it was the right thing to do. I wasn't worried (although my folks probably were), frightened, nervous - none of those things.

Excited? Most probably.

I guess I need to devote a whole chapter to that experience because it was a game-changer for both of us. It helped me to "grow up" - eventually. For Russ it turned out to be valuable experience as a labourer building roads. The official term on his CV would be 'a position in Civil Engineering'! Those experiences - seeing what that particular lifestyle was like, laid the foundations for him developing a career in the cement business.

For me, it even made the local Leicester Mercury newspaper – sort of! I had simply packed in my window-cleaning round and taken off with no word to any of my customers. Street after street of them were used to seeing me up a ladder cleaning away, without fail, every fortnight. One of my older customers in Hartop Road actually wrote to the newspaper to ask if anyone knew where I was! It was if I was a missing person. They worried about me.

Looking back, this was the second of four times I

"made the papers".

The first was a letter I wrote to the TV Times about Clint Eastwood in Rawhide. I was at South Wigston Boys High School and it was a jokey-type account of some cheeky remark Eddie Overton gave to one of our teachers; the third was an actual action shot - caught on camera and printed in the Sports Mercury - from the soccer field. I inadvertently carried the ball under my arm in a game for Cosby United. The fourth, again a photograph, was when I was made a Director for the firm I worked for, David & Charles, in the '80's.

To my shame, the people I really let down when I took off for the Westcountry - not for the first time - were my parents. I seem to recall I didn't even send them a postcard while I was away, leaving them for months on end to worry, without even a word or a phone call.

SO, FINALLY...

Russ and I were on our way to St. Ives – breaking our ties with Blaby and Leicestershire for, eventually, new lives in Devon and Cornwall.

We still live in Devon, individually and with our respective wives; me in South Devon, Russ in North Devon. Over the past 50 years or so we've carved quite different careers and personal lives, but we still keep in touch and will never lose sight of how it all started for us both in 1970.

In so many ways, it was a Golden Year.

But there was one Blaby 'Treasure' we did leave behind...The County Arms - here's a bit of history.

The Union Inn, Glen Parva...before 1937

The Union Inn was next to the Grand Union Canal. Later it was renamed The County Arms when Everards Brewery developed it into a 'Super-Pub' in Art Deco style in 1938. It's now a residential home.

The County Arms (Formerly The Union Inn)

Built in an Art Deco style in 1938, in the 1960's it had two dance floors and this Glen Parva venue hosted local, national and international rock bands and stars of the day.

Little did we know how they would all turn out...

P.S. Another Art Deco pub 'project' was The Airman's Rest - I think it was on the Six Hills Road...not sure.

Chapter Eleven - THE COUNTY ARMS YEARS
No sex, no drugs - just rock 'n' roll - 'onest!

A tribute to an iconic venue not to be forgotten!

In my later teenage years and immediately before I left for the Westcountry, the centre of the universe off the soccer pitch became The County Arms. It was actually in Glen Parva just outside the village of Blaby itself. I was a regular until the end of the 1960s and my early twenties, going at least three nights a week and often more, either with pals or even on my own.

It was the Mecca for live bands - local and some from further afield, including chart-toppers (like Pinkerton's Assorted Colours - ha!), as well as soon-to-be-famous legends like Elton John, Rod Stewart, Jack Bruce and Ginger Baker before they made it. I guess there was plenty of sex and drugs, but it was less obvious then - at least in my circle. Although all of us were as much 'into girls' as you could be, sex wasn't as blatantly shown in the media - TV and Film (there was no internet).

As for drugs, we 'heard about them' - mainly pills within the Mod community - but it didn't become so ingrained into everyday society as it is now, to a level where people's lives and families 'suffered' through drug abuse. At least not on today's scale. Maybe it was becoming more intense within inner cities, but we were yet to see hard drugs like cocaine, heroine and derivatives affecting broader society – and villages.

Up to this time, marijuana seemed to be confined to the jazz and beatnik culture, and American air bases during the war. From the mid-sixties onwards, of course, it became systemic within the hippie culture before filtering into all classes and all sections of society as it is today.

That's how it was perceived within our circle in any case. It may have had stronger influences and presence in larger cities like London, Manchester, Liverpool - and even Birmingham. But not Blaby.

We certainly didn't see it at The County Arms.

I guess every town in the UK had its County Arms -style venue at that time, supporting the emerging British talent spearheaded by The Beatles from 1962 onwards. The main circuit for UK and American touring artists and bands included the Granby Halls and the De Montfort Hall in Leicester itself, where I saw The Beatles (twice), the Rolling Stones, The Animals and many other UK acts as well as American stars such as Dion, Del Shannon, Tommy Roe, Chris Montez and so on. A few years earlier, in 1958 I think it was, my brother was lucky enough to see Buddy Holly.

Getting back to a more local level, as I said, The County Arms was a major player for live bands, where I saw - or guess I might have seen - many solo artists who later became world famous. I mentioned Ginger Baker and Jack Bruce - they were in The Graham Bond Organisation who seemed to feature every 4-5 weeks at The County Arms. As did Zoot Money. Then there was

Long John Baldry and The Steam Packet, another act who I believe, but cannot prove, show-cased Rod Stewart and Reg Dwight, alongside Julie Driscoll and Brian Auger and the Trinity.

Most nights at this Everards Brewery pub they had live music, principally weekends. But Thursday was a 'good night', with (Steve) Fearn's Brass Foundry having a regular slot. Some nights there would be one live band downstairs as well as a disco-style dance going on upstairs.

The County Arms was on the main road into Leicester - nearer Glen Hills than Blaby. It was in walking distance from my house although I drove there when I had a car. The anti 'drink-driving' campaign and the threat of the breathalyser was building momentum but we largely ignored it at first. The social stigma against driving under the influence had not really kicked in.

Most people - including older drivers who resented new rule - drank and drove without any guilt or misgivings at first.

On nights when I didn't go along with Russ or Jarvo or any of my other local pals I would be comfortable enough turning up on my own. There were usually a few girls I knew, or had soon got to know, and I would just spend the evening chatting with them. I still remember one or two.

On Thursdays there was one in particular.

She was a really nice brunette called Joan with whom I would have a dance or two every Thursday, but she would never go out with me on a date. She blew all the guys out after one dance, not just me. (Thank goodness for that!) She was always there with a girlfriend but remained loyal to her regular boyfriend - who we never saw, but she would refer to him 'as her reason' for blowing us out. Even Russ - who was much more attractive to girls than I - fared no better.

Ha! Again, much to my relief!

There was another girl - Jean - I used to see on a regular basis. I actually went out with her on a proper date - once. She eventually blew me out because I got too serious. Too 'heavy'. And she wasn't interested in taking it to the next level.

Jeez. No wonder I was so screwed up!

However, a really special girl who I *nearly* went out with was called Jill (I think) and lived on Western Drive in Blaby - on the council estate. She reminded me of Jean Shrimpton - the #1 model of the day. One night we were sat talking, just we two, waiting for Graham Bond and the band to arrive. Our table was on the edge facing the dance floor. Patio glass doors leading onto the car park below the dance floor were immediately behind us, where we sat. Suddenly the doors burst open. Bang!

Two guys brushed past us.

What I thought were a couple of ruffians - long hair and scruffy - strode across the floor to the stage. They had purpose in mind. But what? The stage and instruments were set up ready for the band. We stopped talking and just stared, bracing ourselves in case of trouble. We were expecting the worst. Then one of them sat himself down behind the drums and began to play. Loud. Then we realised. Phew! Not to worry.

It turned out to be Ginger Baker! The other - on bass - was Jack Bruce.

Back to Jill again for one moment.

I said I 'nearly' went out with her. True, she did agree to go out with me, separate from seeing her at The County Arms but, a couple of days before we were due to meet there was a knock on our front door. I opened it and there she was, as pretty as ever.

But with bad news.

"I'm sorry," she began," but I can't go out with you."

She said no more and, to this day, I have no idea why. Neither did I say anything - not a word, apart from perhaps, "OK" as she turned to go. I stood watching her walk away down our drive. I closed the door slowly. I doubt whether she looked back.

"Who was that, John?" came a voice from the kitchen.

"Nobody, mam."

My point is - yes, I was disappointed, but I admired her *so much* for having the decency to say beforehand she wouldn't go out with me, rather than 'stand me up' on the night - which did happen to me a couple of times with other girls. You always felt a right pillock, having put on your best clothes, got on the bus to town, standing patiently at the Clock Tower (or wherever you'd agreed to meet) at the appointed hour - only to be still there twenty minutes later, after a 'no show'.

Talking of dress, as I recall, denim jeans were usually out of the question. It was trousers, proper shoes (no trainers) and a shirt - even a tie and jacket, sometimes. That was just to go to the pub, and most certainly if you went dancing. One time, to really make an impression, I remember doing something quite ridiculous when I look back on it.

The 'Mod' scene was strong. Whilst we were all *influenced* by it, I cannot class myself *as* a mod. However, a really cool guy - a fellow soccer player in Russ's youth team, Mick O'Gleby - came with us one night to The County Arms. He was sporting a really elegant brown (or was it black?) 'full length leather'.

Coat - that is.

It must have been a Thursday because - you guessed it - 'Joan' was there, dancing as usual with her friend. And, also as usual, guys would go up to her, get one dance, only to be blown out. Then I had an idea.

'This could tip the balance with Joan' I thought.

I asked Mick if I could borrow his coat - he said yes, of course. Up I got, put on his 'full length leather', ready to wow Joan with my outfit - by dancing in it!

Did it work?

No!

Did I look a pillock?

Probably.

But, hey, you have to try everything. Right?

Earlier I mentioned The Beatles.

The second time I saw them they'd really 'made it'

and (female) fans screamed the place down during live concerts - so much so that you simply couldn't hear them. That was after queueing from 11pm Saturday night to 10am Sunday morning for tickets. We stood on a cold pavement in Leicester city centre, four deep, until the booking office opened.

It was a waste of time and money.

The first time I saw them it was different.

I treated a local girl from the village to a ticket, buying myself a new jacket, trousers, shirt, tie and shoes to take her out. The performance was very calm and sedate in comparison to a later concert, with no screaming fans. The irony was - nearly 60 years later - I received a knock back. I saw a post from the girl on a Facebook page and dropped her a note to remind her of our 'date'. Amazingly - although I have to laugh at myself - *she denied it.* She said it wasn't me who took her to the show, claiming she went with her dad. Little Eva was also on the bill.

Now, I know I was always well mannered and respectful on a first date but, to be mistaken for the girl's Dad is a bit rich, don't you think?

She also got the Little Eva bit wrong.

It was our only date, though...

At an even more local level, the dances at The Social Centre were not to be missed when they featured live music by 'The Primates', later to be called 'The Four Sights'. Dougie Abbot on rhythm guitar, Tim Airey on bass, Dave Lindsey on drums and vocals, and Bill Coleman on lead guitar was the line-up.

It was they who inspired Melv and I to start a group. Their covers were excellent, particularly when they replicated the latest Friday single release by The Beatles on the very next Saturday dance, note perfect.

How did they manage that?

As it turned out, Bill's sister, Bess, was PA to The Beatles at the time. Paul McCartney is reported to have said, "Bess never sold us out." A music journalist and true professional, I understand Bess sadly died a few years ago in Australia.

She's another who deserves recognition.

Sadly, it would appear that The Four Sights broke up after a year or two, not sure why. After going to the USA, someone suggested they market themselves as 'The London Knights'. Later, Bill went on to play with leading jazz bands, I think Acker Bilk, Chris Barber, and Kenny Ball (but I could have some of that detail wrong). He's moved on from lead guitar to double bass - and he still plays every Sunday lunchtime at a pub in Rutland (at least, he did the last I heard).

Other bands who have emerged from Leicester are, of course, Kasabian - but long after The County Arms days. Both Russ and I - but Russ more than me - played soccer with Sergio Pizzorno's dad in Blaby on Northfield Park, and Russ and he later played for Blaby Boys' Club.

John Deacon of Queen is also an Oadby lad. I think I read somewhere that John's earlier band's first gig was at Enderby Town Hall. Ironically, when Melv and I formed the four-piece 'Denhams', that was *our* first dance at which we played. I think we only had about fifty minutes playlist so, after a ten-minute break, we repeated the first set in the second half! And lived!

And still got paid.

A Leicester band that seemed to go on to develop a cult following was 'Legay' - later renamed 'Gypsy'. I remember them as 'Legay' and that they were loud! But the other thing I also recall was that one of the band member's dads *was our bread delivery guy*. For Mother's Pride. He was SO proud of his boy.

Perhaps we should have called it Father's Pride! Ha!

I mentioned The County Arms as being on a circuit for emerging acts. Of course, the 'biggy' as a London venue was always Eel Pie Island. 'Gypsy' were on that bill at one of its festivals, way back.

That sort of wraps up the rock and roll scene as far as my personal experience goes, but I couldn't leave the subject without mentioning The Granby Halls again and The Il Rondo. The latter was an out-and-out Mod hang-out. Both were favourites with The Who, who I saw live at a Leicester University Rag Week Ball. I remember dancing just feet away from the band on stage. Amazing that they played in front of thousands and thousands at Woodstock just a year or two later.

Earlier I mentioned the band that Melv and I started.

We lasted about a year, as I recall, but we badly needed a good musician mentor to improve our performances to survive. We learnt the songs from books of lyrics we bought for nine pence at WH Smiths. There was no online source - no internet - and no YouTube to learn from. As well as musicianship, we lacked equipment - good amplifiers and such. But we played at a few dances and parties - even once at a Leicester University Saturday night dance!

It was another 45 years or so after the break-up before I picked up the guitar to play again seriously. Since 2013 I've made it one of my current daily passions - occasionally playing in our local band - the Teignagers. If only I hadn't packed it in *as a teenager* I might have made something of myself.

I left Leicester in 1970 to eventually settle in Devon so, thankfully, I didn't witness the decline of The County Arms. Several years afterwards it closed, went into disrepair and, more recently, it has been converted into assisted living for pensioners. Amazing! If I still lived in Leicester I might have seen myself ending up in one of those apartments before long.

Home from Home!

But this time I might be armed with a nice collection of guitars and musical partners for jam sessions!

~ *** ~

This must be continued...one day.

Epilogue

This is as far as I'm taking you today, on my journey through life. It's been a life with two halves.

The first half was the first twenty four years when I lived with my parents, in Blaby. I would have added 'growing up', but I didn't really mature until I left mother's apron strings to seek adventure and a different lifestyle in the Westcountry.

Devon and Cornwall initially, then Devon almost exclusively from age thirty until now, at seventy eight.

As with most septegenarians, life has had its ups and downs, but I remember the first two decades on this earth most fondly. Yes, from a personal perspective but also, more importantly, because I consider the immediate post war (WW2) period as being a time that should not be fotrgotten, and that history books should not ignore.

So, forgive me where I seem to have been too self-indulgent. I couldn't have written this without lapsing into personal anecdotes. But I do hope that you can picture events of my own life within a wider context. That of life in general from the late 1940's until 1970.

Much of that context may now be faded, or lost...but it's certainly not forgotten.

Not by me.

Further reading of the works by J S Morey

Read My Shorts: from which The Coal-Miner's Son is taken, together with a collection of stories in prose and verse.

Three Easy Pieces: two romances and one haunting tale

Unresolved?: Death on honeymoon in St Ives, Cornwall

The Sign of the Rose: Book 1 of the historical romantic, Romani saga - a journey from Ireland to England, late 1800's
The Black Rose of Blaby: Book 2, in a Leicestershire village where historical facts blur with mystical events
Rose: The Missing Years and Finding Rose: two novels; one story; told from two perspectives - Books 3 & 4 in the saga

Those Italian Girls: a murder/mystery/romance set in the Tuscan wine-rowing town of Volterra

Wild Hearts Roam Free: modern-day 1960's pioneers seek a new life, and find themselves, in the grasslands of Wyoming
Wild Heart Come Home: celebrating the life and times of those sharing Lakota heritage and a one-ness of spirit

Visit our website - newnovel.co.uk for updates

Keep in touch through my Amazon Author Page

Printed in Great Britain
by Amazon